The Presbyterian Predicament

THE PRESBYTERIAN PRESENCE:
THE TWENTIETH-CENTURY EXPERIENCE

Series Editors

Milton J Coalter

John M. Mulder

Louis B. Weeks

The Presbyterian Predicament: Six Perspectives

Edited by

Milton J Coalter

John M. Mulder

Louis B. Weeks

Essays by

Robert Wuthnow, Edward W. Farley,

Barbara G. Wheeler, Benton Johnson,

Gayraud S. Wilmore, and

Barbara Brown Zikmund

Westminster/John Knox Press
Louisville, Kentucky

Scripture quotations from the Revised Standard Version of the Bible are copyrighted 1946, 1952, ©1971, 1973 by the Division of Christian Education of the National Council of the Churches of Christ in the U.S.A. and are used by permission.

Chapter 1, "The Restructuring of American Presbyterianism," by Robert Wuthnow, appears in a different form in his book *The Struggle for America's Soul* (Grand Rapids: Wm. B. Eerdmans Publishing Co., 1989).

Book design by Gene Harris

First edition

Published by Westminster/John Knox Press
Louisville, Kentucky

PRINTED IN THE UNITED STATES OF AMERICA

9 8 7 6 5 4 3 2 1

Library of Congress Cataloging-in-Publication Data

The Presbyterian predicament : six perspectives / edited by Milton J. Coalter, John M. Mulder, Louis B. Weeks ; essays by Robert Wuthnow . . . [et al.] — 1st ed.
        p.   cm. — (The Presbyterian presence : the twentieth-century experience)
   Includes bibliographical references.
   ISBN 0-664-25097-1

   1. Presbyterian Church—United States—History—20th century.
2. Presbyterian Church (U.S.A.)—History. 3. Reformed Church—United States—History—20th century. 4. United States—Church history—20th century. I. Coalter, Milton J. II. Mulder, John M., 1946–   . III. Weeks, Louis, 1941–   . IV. Wuthnow, Robert.
V. Series: Presbyterian presence.
BX8937.P78 1990
285'.13—dc20   89-29105
                                                                              CIP

Contents

Series Foreword

This series, "The Presbyterian Presence: The Twentieth-Century Experience," is the product of a significant research project analyzing American Presbyterianism in this century. Funded by the Lilly Endowment and based at Louisville Presbyterian Theological Seminary, the project is part of a broader research effort that analyzes the history of mainstream Protestantism. By analyzing American Presbyterianism as a case study, we hope not only to chronicle its fate in the twentieth-century but also to illumine larger patterns of religious change in mainstream Protestantism and in American religious and cultural life.

This case study of American Presbyterianism and the broader research on mainstream Protestantism arise out of an epochal change in American religion that has occurred during the twentieth century. Mainstream American Protestantism refers to those churches that emerged from the American Revolution as the dominant Protestant bodies and were highly influential in shaping American religion and culture during the nineteenth century. It includes the Presbyterians, Episcopalians, Methodists, Congregationalists (now the United Church of Christ), Disciples, and American or northern Baptists.

In this century, these churches have been displaced—religiously and culturally—to a significant degree. All have suffered severe membership losses since the 1960s. All have experienced significant theological tensions and shifts in emphasis. All are characterized by problems in their organization as institutions. And yet they remain influential voices in the spectrum of American religion and retain an enduring vitality in the face of a massive reconfiguration of American religious life.

The result is a complex phenomenon that is not easily described. Some would say the term "mainstream" or "mainline" is itself suspect and embodies ethnocentric and elitist assumptions. What characterized American religious history, they argue, was its diversity and its pluralism. Some groups may have believed they were religiously or culturally dominant, but the historical reality is much more pluralistic. Others would maintain that if there was a "mainstream," it no longer exists. Still others would propose that the mainstream itself has changed. The denominations of the evangelical awakening of the nineteenth century have been replaced by the evangelical churches of the late twentieth century—Southern Baptist, charismatic, Pentecostal.

Some propose that the term "mainline" or "mainstream" should be dropped in favor of talking about "liberal" Protestantism, but such a change presents additional problems. Like "evangelical," the term "liberal" is an extremely vague word to describe a set of Christian beliefs, values, and behavior. Furthermore, virtually all the "mainstream" churches contain large numbers of people who would describe themselves as either evangelical or liberal, thus making it very difficult to generalize about them as a denomination.

Despite the debates about terminology and the categories for analyzing American Protestantism, there is general agreement that American culture and American Protestantism of the late twentieth century are very different from what they were in the late nineteenth century. What has changed is the religious and cultural impact of Ameri-

can Protestantism. A study of American Presbyterianism
is a good lens for examining that change, for in spite of
their relatively small numbers, Presbyterians are, or were,
quintessential mainstreamers, exerting a great deal of influence because of their economic, social, educational, and
cultural advantages.

When did the change occur? In a pioneering article written more than fifty years ago, Arthur M. Schlesinger, Sr.,
pointed to the period from 1875 to 1900 as "a critical
period" in American religion. In particular, American
Protestants confronted the external challenges of immigra-
tion, industrialization, and urbanization and the internal
challenges posed by Darwinism, biblical criticism, history
of religions, and the new social sciences.[1] Robert T. Handy
has maintained that the 1920s witnessed a "religious depression." The result was a "second disestablishment" of
American Protestantism. When the churches lost legal establishment in the U.S. Constitution, they attempted to
"Christianize" American culture.[2] But by the 1920s, it was
clear that both legal and cultural establishment had been
rejected. Sydney Ahlstrom points to the 1960s as the time
when American religion and culture took a "radical turn"
and the "Puritan culture" of the United States was shattered.[3] Wade Clark Roof and William McKinney build on
Ahlstrom's argument, proposing that the 1960s and 1970s
represent a "third disestablishment" in which mainstream
churches lost their religious dominance.[4]

These diverse interpretations underscore the fact that
the crises of mainstream Protestantism did not appear
suddenly and that the developments within one tradition—American Presbyterianism—are mirrored in other
denominations as well. While some of our studies reach
back into the late nineteenth century, most of our studies
focus on the period after the fundamentalist controversy
within Presbyterianism during the 1920s and 1930s. For a
variety of reasons, that became a watershed for Presbyterians and ushered in the twentieth century.

The value of this substantial Presbyterian case study can
be seen from at least two perspectives. First, this research

is designed to write a chapter in the history of American religion and culture. It is the story of the attempt of one tradition—its people and its institutions—to respond to the crosscurrents of the twentieth century. Second, it is an attempt to illumine the problems and predicaments of American Presbyterianism so that its members and leaders might better understand the past as a resource for its future direction.

The series title was carefully chosen. Presence is more than passive existence, and it connotes the landmark that we hope these groups of studies provide for comparing the equally important pilgrimages of other mainline Protestant denominations through the past century. Missiologists have characterized the Christian responsibility as one of "profound presence" in the world, patterned on the presence of God in providence, in the incarnation, and in the work of the Holy Spirit. In the words of missionary and theologian John V. Taylor, Christians "stand" in the world in the name of Christ to be "really and totally present in the present."[5]

Has the Presbyterian presence declined into mere existence? Have the commitments of Presbyterians degenerated into lifeless obligations? What forces have informed, transformed, or deformed our distinctive presence within the Christian community and the society? And can changes in Presbyterianism invigorate their continued yearnings to represent Christ in the world today? These are the questions posed in the series and the queries addressed by the Caldwell Lectures at Louisville Seminary from quite different perspectives.

More than sixty researchers, plus students at Louisville Seminary and generous colleagues in seminaries, colleges, and universities throughout the United States, have cooperated in the research on American Presbyterianism. Many are historians, but others are sociologists, economists, musicians, theologians, pastors, and lay people. What has excited us as a research team was the opportunity of working on a fascinating historical problem with critical implications for the Presbyterian Church and mainstream Protestantism. Animating our work and conversations was the hope that this research might make a difference, that it might help one church and a broader Christian tradition understand the problems more clearly so that its witness might be more faithful. It is with this hope that we issue this series, "The Presbyterian Presence: The Twentieth-Century Experience."

Milton J Coalter
John M. Mulder
Louis B. Weeks

Acknowledgments

Previous drafts of the following essays were delivered in 1989 as part of the Caldwell Lectures at Louisville Presbyterian Theological Seminary. This series was in honor of Dr. Frank H. Caldwell, who served as President from 1936 to 1964 and as Professor of Homiletics from 1930 to 1964.

We want to thank all those who helped make these lectures possible, especially Barbara Tesorero, Director of Continuing and Lay Education; her assistant, Judith Elkin; and Norma Porterfield, Director of the Office of Information. This project has been made immeasurably easier by the assistance of our secretaries—Beverly Hourigan, Kem Longino, Dana Rohde, and Ingrid Tanghe.

We are also grateful to our colleagues at Louisville Seminary for their encouragement and support, and to the Board of Directors for generously allowing each of us time to carry out the research and planning for this series.

We are pleased to be working with the newly merged Westminster/John Knox Press in bringing this volume and the series to publication. We appreciate the help that Publisher Robert McIntyre and Editorial Director Davis Perkins have provided to us.

This project would not have been possible without the

financial support of the Lilly Endowment and the creative stimulation provided by Dr. Robert Wood Lynn, Senior Vice President for Religion. Bob retired in mid-1989, but it was his vision that prompted the research on American mainstream Protestantism. For his wise advice, patience, and encouragement we are deeply grateful. He has been and continues to be a perceptive mentor and a discerning critic.

Contributors

Edward W. Farley is Professor of Theology at the Divinity School of Vanderbilt University. His numerous theological works include *The Fragility of Knowledge: Theological Education in the Church and the University; Theologia: The Fragmentation and Unity of Theological Education; Ecclesial Reflection: An Anatomy of Theological Method*; and *Ecclesial Man: A Social Phenomenology of Faith and Reason.*

Benton Johnson is Professor of Sociology at the University of Oregon. He has written extensively on mainline Protestantism, his most recent publications being "Is There Hope for Liberal Protestantism?" in *Mainline Protestantism in the Twentieth Century: Its Problems and Prospects* and "Winning Lost Sheep: A Recovery Course for Liberal Protestantism" in *Liberal Protestantism: Realities and Possibilities.*

Barbara G. Wheeler is President of Auburn Theological Seminary and was formerly the Director of the Women's Theological Coalition of the Boston Theological Institute. A researcher and consultant, she has conducted studies on clergy continuing education, Doctor of Ministry programs, and religious publishing. She is the editor of James F.

Hopewell's *Congregation: Stories and Structures* and co-editor with Joseph C. Hough of *Beyond Clericalism: The Congregation as a Focus for Theological Education.*

Gayraud S. Wilmore, Distinguished Visiting Professor at the Interdenominational Theological Center, Atlanta, recently retired as Professor of Afro-American Religious Studies and Dean at New York Theological Seminary. Dr. Wilmore is a prolific commentator on the Black Christian experience and particularly on the situation of African Americans in predominantly white denominations. Among his many publications are *Black and Presbyterian, Black Religion and Black Radicalism,* and *Black Theology: A Documentary History, 1966–1979.*

Robert Wuthnow is Professor of Sociology at Princeton University. His research on the sociology of religion has resulted in many articles and books. Among his most recent works are *The Struggle for America's Soul* and *The Restructuring of American Religion: Society and Faith Since World War II.*

Barbara Brown Zikmund is the Dean and Professor of Church History at the Pacific School of Religion. She is active in feminist scholarship and in the United Church of Christ, in which she is an ordained minister. Her publications include *Hidden Histories in the United Church of Christ* and *Discovering the Church.* She served as President of the Association of Theological Schools from 1988 to 1990.

Introduction

Alongside Caldwell Chapel at Louisville Presbyterian Theological Seminary there stands the figure of a crowing rooster. Spare and modern in form, the brass sculpture recalls an ancient Christian symbol of warning. Three times the cock's crow signaled Peter's repeated betrayal of his discipleship.

Despite the vitality of many congregations throughout the Presbyterian Church (U.S.A.), a number of sustained mission efforts at presbytery, synod, and assembly levels, and the dedication of thousands of faithful members, several elements of the denomination's present situation renew the rooster's poignant cry of caution. The loss in membership, a perceived spiritual malaise throughout much of the church, and the widely voiced perception that serious theology has not characterized the Presbyterian Church's recent history trouble the prospects for the church's future vitality. These factors also provide the context for the 1989 Caldwell Lectures offered in this book.

The situation in the Presbyterian Church (U.S.A.) is similar to the condition of other mainline Protestant bodies. Wade Clark Roof and William McKinney have surveyed these broad patterns in contemporary America in

American Mainline Religion. Robert Wuthnow, in *The Re-structuring of American Religion,* insightfully delineates the forces at work that diminish the cultural influence traditionally enjoyed by mainline communions.[1] But what special ingredients characterize the Presbyterians' predicaments and prospects? How do these relate to the problems of other churches? What insights into these futures can be seen?

The Presbyterian Church (U.S.A.), through its reunion of the two largest strands in American Presbyterianism, represents an important historical presence within the nation's Christian community. Both in the colonial period and in the new United States of America, the Presbyterians were an energetic and influential force in the society. Vehement disagreements over the sequence of ministerial education, the need for subscription to confessional standards, the nature of biblical authority, and the strategies for mission occasioned several divisions from the first Presbyterian denomination. But conflict at the time of the Civil War generated the most fierce and pernicious schism. In 1906 the so-called northern Presbyterians reunited with a majority of the Cumberland Presbyterian Church and significant numbers of Black members and congregations in the South. This gave the Presbyterian Church in the U.S.A. a national presence throughout the twentieth century. A later union with the United Presbyterian Church in North America during 1956 made the resulting United Presbyterian Church in the U.S.A. (UPCUSA) the largest Presbyterian body in this country. Finally, the century-old division between North and South was healed in 1983 with the forging of the Presbyterian Church in the U.S. and the UPCUSA into the present Presbyterian Church (U.S.A.).

This initial volume in the series "The Presbyterian Presence: The Twentieth-Century Experience" is the firstfruits of a major research project on American Presbyterianism in this century. The essays were originally presented as the Caldwell Lectures at Louisville Seminary in March 1989. Support of these lectures and the research that will appear in this series was provided by the Lilly Endowment and Louisville Seminary.

Several terms have been used by scholars to characterize the present situation of the Presbyterian Church and its "mainline" Protestant companions. Decline, malaise, division, and demise are only a few of those currently employed. However, the word "predicament" in this volume's title better encapsulates the peculiar dilemma of Presbyterians in the last decade of the twentieth century. Rather than being infected with decay or shattered by schism, the denomination seems stymied, and sometimes immobilized, by the conflicting consequences of sets of parallel allegiances and commitments. Presbyterians have, for instance, traditionally spurned a sectarian isolation from their host culture, yet they now recognize secularizing tendencies in that contemporary milieu that threaten the very vitality of their faith. Presbyterians long strived to bring new souls into their fellowship, but some Presbyterians worry now that recent emphases on evangelism in service to membership loss may mitigate longstanding commitments to social witness. Similarly, attempts of late to foster inclusive decision-making have, on occasion, frustrated Presbyterian decisions being made with dispatch. Likewise, a desire to instill a distinctive Presbyterian identity that sustains membership participation and loyalty often conflicts with the church's persistent identification with the ecumenical movement.

These and other predicaments the lecturers in this book were asked to address as they took the common theme "The Predicaments and Prospects for Presbyterians." In each case, they approached their subject from vastly different angles and out of their diverse disciplines.

Robert Wuthnow, a sociologist at Princeton University, traces the source of Presbyterian troubles to the decline of American denominationalism generally. Presbyterians have experienced more than their fair share of ecclesiastical battles and interest-group activity. But their situation today does not differ appreciably from that of other denominations. Wuthnow states that multiple, complex

social forces and competing worldviews within denominational boundaries have disrupted and debilitated connec-
tional allegiances.

Distinctive qualities and perspectives seem to be disap-
pearing rapidly in traditional mainline denominations.
Though Presbyterians are still more likely to have attended college or to belong to a recognized profession in
society than members of any other Protestant denomination except the Episcopal Church, the differences have become statistically less significant, and the trend points to
even smaller differences in the future. Likewise, a rise in
cultural tolerance relieves past social pressure on members
of other denominations to "switch" to the Presbyterian
Church.

Wuthnow examines the struggle between liberals and
conservatives in the Presbyterian Church (U.S.A.) and argues that the division has grown in recent decades. He
highlights the development of single-interest groups, or
what he characterizes as "struggle groups." Such groups
exist to contend with other single-interest groups within
the denomination; mission programs beyond their particular concerns take second priority, if any at all, in their
agenda. Struggle groups have proliferated at presbytery,
synod, and denominational levels, causing further weakening of identity and fragmenting of energy in the Presbyterian communion.

As for the future of the Presbyterian Church (U.S.A.),
Wuthnow does not present much cause for celebration. He
describes a current pattern of college-educated Americans
frequently withdrawing from corporate religious activity at
the very time that birthrates among the Presbyterians continue to drop.

Wuthnow suggests that liberals and conservatives should
find avenues of reconciliation. At the least, each should not
blame the other for causing numerical decline and other
woes of the church. He considers the theology of reconciliation, which lies at the core of the Christian faith, an important rationale for such healing activity.

Edward Farley, a theologian at Vanderbilt University

and a graduate of Louisville Seminary, summarizes the Presbyterians' dilemma and then urges that they sustain the theological stance that already characterizes their life as he understands it. Farley advocates that the Presbyterian Church (U.S.A.) affirm and exploit its "critical modernism."

"Modernism," the early-twentieth-century theological alternative to fundamentalism, carries some helpful ambiguities for Farley. It can designate the most liberal wing of Protestantism, while theologically it can also name those willing to reconcile an ancient gospel with current realities. Secular or cultural modernism feeds on fads and adopts new techniques and technologies unreflectively. Critical modernism remains responsive to modernity but selectively accepts categories presented by the contemporary world. The Presbyterian Church (U.S.A.) now carries a critical modernist worldview, according to Farley, and to retreat from this stance would be both strategically ill-advised and spiritually inauthentic to the present challenges of the gospel.

Farley lists six areas in which critical modernism can be discerned and formulates theological questions raised by each. He points to the malleability of Reformed or Calvinist theology, the relativity of confessions and creeds of the communion, and the propriety of the historical-critical method as a part of biblical study. He cites the compatibility of religious truth with truth claims made in other arenas of human knowledge, the pluralistic nature of the Christian church, and the gospel's social implications. Most Presbyterians affirm the subjects encapsulated in Farley's set of questions, and Farley suggests that together this cluster of convictions constitutes a precious resource within the Christian movement, i.e., a critical modernist posture of enduring value to the whole of the church.

Farley insists that, in order to preserve its unique perspective, the Presbyterian Church (U.S.A.) take Reformed and Calvinist themes more seriously by drawing out scriptural and confessional implications from the contemporary culture. He advocates a program of serious biblical and theological study for young people. In his view, the current educational programs offer little more than diluted traditionalist emphases. Moreover, he calls on Presbyterians and other critical modernists not to mimic other portions of the Christian family because they seem more "successful" numerically.

Barbara Wheeler, President of Auburn Theological Seminary and a leader among theological educators in the study of congregational identity, addresses the character of Presbyterian "particular churches," as congregations are termed within the Presbyterian Church. She develops a typology of scholarly theories for understanding congregational dynamics, and she identifies three theoretical structures by which the nature of Protestant congregations has been and is being explored. In works by Stephen Warner, Dean Kelley, and others, congregations are seen as passive entities, receiving identity chiefly from external sources and alternating between high and routine energy levels controlled by outside forces. She terms this the "wineskin" theory.

Works by James Hopewell, Nancy Ammerman, and Melvin Williams claim that each congregation bears a special identity, a peculiar stamp, a dynamic and self-selected story. Hopewell even uses the term "mythology" to denote this congregational self-understanding. This singular identity is imprinted almost indelibly on a congregation by events that it experiences and later selectively chooses to chronicle in a remembered story of who its fellowship is. This theory Wheeler calls the "cultural" view.

A third theory she finds in the work of Michael Ducey Ducey asserted that congregations need leadership, but "charisma" can come from a variety of sources. The people and their pastor(s) together "choose," perhaps informally and even unconsciously, whether their congregation will endure and whether they will become catalysts for forming a culture that will remain after they are gone. Wheeler calls this the "voluntary" theory.

Wheeler urges Presbyterians to look to congregational life in the face of mainline decline, employing particularly the "cultural" and "voluntary" perspectives for under-standing these little-studied forms of communal religious life. Congregations can be transformed, she asserts, and they can become, if they are not already, primary carriers of vital Presbyterian traditions. She also advocates much more attention to the training of congregational leader-ship, both lay and clergy.

In a quite different vein, Benton Johnson's lecture exam-ines the demise of a Presbyterian "institution," Sabbath observance, as an indicator of the broader diffusion of the church's religious identity. According to Johnson, a sociol-ogist at the University of Oregon, spiritual practice, to-gether with teaching and morality, is one of the three pillars of a religious tradition. Sabbath observance com-prised the center of spiritual practice for Presbyterians at the beginning of the twentieth century, even though signs of its eventual demise were already evident. Presbyterians believed that the Sabbath represented an occasion for the worship of God and instruction in church school as it does today. But it also offered the opportunity for people to synchronize their life patterns with the hebdomadal struc-ture of creation in which God made the world in six days and rested the seventh. Nations that honored the Sabbath would remain healthy; people who refrained from Sabbath desecration would be prepared for God's kingdom. For Presbyterians in particular, the Sabbath embodied a seri-ous ethical stance that linked personal and corporate mo-rality as well as a range of moral practices that Johnson terms "the old agenda." That "old agenda" included, among other things, instruction in scripture and cate-chisms, modest dress, avoidance of worldly amusements, and abstinence from alcohol.

The decline of Sabbath observance proceeded by stages, and Johnson outlines several steps suggested in reports to General Assemblies of the Presbyterian Church in the U.S. and the Presbyterian Church in the U.S.A. He finds that systemic and institutional Sabbath observance in the northern church had dissipated by 1960. In that year a General Assembly pronouncement advocated civil libertarian values over traditional Presbyterian emphases. In the PCUSA, a similar course led to a 1958 pronouncement which suggested that people use Christian judgment in discerning the appropriate use of Sunday for worship and study, recreation, and family life.

Johnson strongly urges attention to matters of spiritual practice in the Presbyterian Church (U.S.A.) today. He argues that without such patterns of piety, moral disciplines and Christian education stand little chance of survival. Further, he suggests resurrecting discussion about the Sabbath as a matter for corporate and personal attention by Presbyterians.

Historian Gayraud Wilmore of the Interdenominational Theological Center chronicles the journey of Black Presbyterians through the twentieth century, pointing to the deep ambivalence that accompanied their participation. The prized value of Black identity has lived sometimes uncomfortably alongside Black Presbyterians' vision of a racially inclusive church in an integrated society.

According to Wilmore, Black Presbyterians began their formal caucusing under theologically conservative leaders like John W. Lee and Francis J. Grimké. An Afro-American Presbyterian Council, dedicated to seeking Black equality of opportunity with white Presbyterians, began in 1894. Black Presbyterians in the Presbyterian Church U.S.A. apparently accepted the "separate but equal" fiction of American segregationism embodied in racially identifiable judicatories. A short-lived Afro-American Presbyterian Church began in the Presbyterian Church U.S., but it quickly followed the northern pattern of a separate, racially defined governing body under the one white-controlled General Assembly.

Black Presbyterians chose the ambiguity of participation in a predominantly white denomination over independence and a separate identity in the Reformed family. While the integrationist model prevailed for the AAPC, a segregationist model continued to appeal to the racially identifiable governing bodies. When the civil rights movement occupied the consciousness of Black Presbyterians and their white allies, Wilmore says, the nature of the ambiguity changed somewhat; but the tension of upholding Black identity while promoting a more inclusive church continued.

In the midst of the civil rights movement, the UPCUSA became the first major, predominantly white denomination to appoint Black-led staff with some authority. Black Presbyterians in that denomination also organized Concerned Presbyterians, a successor to the AAPC, and the newly born Presbyterian Interracial Council had much to do with the election of the first Black moderator of the church, Edler Hawkins, in 1964.

The PCUS, moving a bit more slowly than its more national sibling, created the Council on Church and Race and appointed Black leadership for it in 1970. A year later Black southern Presbyterians started their own caucus.

Wilmore muses on the strong efforts of the major Presbyterian bodies in the 1960s and early 1970s to combat racism in their midst and considers why interracial gains and hopes represented in the serious Black presence in Presbyterian leadership positions did not seem to prevail more thoroughly than it has. While noting the ambiguity of the Black minority in a white church, he calls upon Blacks to transcend it and upon white "allies" to understand and support Blacks as they cope with it.

Barbara Brown Zikmund, a historian and Dean of the Pacific School of Religion, examines the nature of ordination and how its theology changed under the unprecedented impact of women entering the ministry.

Zikmund points out that ordination arose out of the need to designate local representatives as recipients of wider, apostolic authority and to formalize the avenues of historic witness to the gospel. Ordination became a means of protecting the Christian community from heresy, and increasingly the ordained assumed civic responsibility as Christianity became a state religion. Over time, ordination was intimately linked with the mysteries of the sacraments and acquired an objective character in the minds of Christians.

Among Reformed Christians, a middle way between dependence on clerical leadership and lay control has been strengthened by the relatively recent ordination of significant numbers of women. Although tempted like men to invest primarily in a "professional" identity, women may more readily overcome this temptation as they emphasize human relationships. American women ministers have different concerns and questions regarding the nature and use of power. Zikmund indicates that the sharing of ordained leadership by women and men in the Presbyterian Church (U.S.A.) may lead to a broadening of the ministry of the Word to include a greater emphasis on teaching as well as preaching and concentration on baptism as much as the Eucharist in the life of the church. She hopes that the priesthood of all believers will be enhanced in the process.

Vigorous discussion with each of the lecturers followed their respective presentations. During the "talk-back times," lay people, pastors, seminary students, and faculty reflected on the practical implications of the lectures for programs in the Presbyterian Church (U.S.A.) and other denominations. The lecturers frequently reflected questions back to their questioners, thereby expressing the hope that all would cooperate in overcoming the numerical decline if possible, but certainly in seeking renewed energy and vigor for Christian witness and in thinking constructively about God's relationship with humanity and with the whole creation. In the words of Gayraud Wilmore, "We are all in this Christian community together. We need to listen and to respond faithfully in this time God gives to us."

We earnestly hope the dialogue engendered by the lectures at the "talk-back times" will continue for the readers of these essays. The Presbyterian Church (U.S.A.) can only benefit from serious scrutiny by these perceptive scholars.

Milton J Coalter
John M. Mulder
Louis B. Weeks

1

The Restructuring
of American Presbyterianism:
Turmoil in One Denomination

Robert Wuthnow

In my book *The Restructuring of American Religion,* I attempted to outline some of the broad contours of religious change in the nation at large over the past four decades.[1] Starting with the years immediately after World War II, and taking some long retrospective glances at the development of American religion prior to the war, I attempted to describe the institutional and cultural climate of American religion in the 1940s and 1950s, showing some of the preconditions that were to reinforce later conflicts, and then tracing the trajectory of these conflicts into the 1980s and suggesting some of their cultural and political implications. Here I would like to consider the ways in which Presbyterianism reflects these broader patterns, how it may depart from them, and what the turmoil it presently faces may suggest for its clergy and members in the immediate future.

In one sense, of course, Presbyterians are not a typical case. Presbyterians have a long history of internal conflict, and for this reason the current cleavage between liberals and conservatives that we shall be considering may represent less of a restructuring for Presbyterianism than it does for American religion more generally.

The conflicts and schisms that have characterized Presbyterian history are well known. No sooner had the first General Presbytery been founded in Philadelphia in 1706 than tensions began to erupt. Conservatives, largely consisting of recent Scottish and Scotch-Irish immigrants to Pennsylvania, argued that membership and church discipline should be contingent on strict adherence to the Westminster Confession; liberals, who tended to be concentrated more in the New York and New England presbyteries, argued that the Bible alone was a sufficient rule of faith and practice.

After several attempts at compromise and reconciliation in the 1720s, the conflict grew more intense with the advent of revivalism and an emphasis on personal conversion that developed during the Great Awakening. The more liberal "New Side," as it was called, preached revivalism and an experiential knowledge of Christ, while the "Old Side" stood for a more corporatist form of church discipline rooted in the Westminster tradition. Each side claimed authority in matters of doctrine and clergy training, and both sides institutionalized their claims in concrete organizations.

Conflict between Old School and New School Presbyterians erupted again with considerable intensity during the first half of the nineteenth century. Revivalism and the Reformed tradition in doctrine and church government, control of mission boards, and cooperation with other denominations in ventures such as the founding of Union Theological Seminary in New York City in 1836 served as foci of contention. The two factions officially split from each other in 1837 and remained divided until 1869. Meanwhile, other schisms were also dividing Presbyterians into a more diverse range of denominations. There was the founding of the Cumberland Presbyterian Church in 1810, the 1833 split between the Reformed Presbyterian Church, General Synod, and the Reformed Presbyterian Church of North America, and the formation of the Presbyterian Church U.S. in the South at the outset of the Civil War.[2]

In the twentieth century, Presbyterians' involvement in the conflict between fundamentalists and modernists again sets their history apart from that of many other denominations. The conflict was particularly intense among Presbyterians because it revolved around a number of hotly contested issues: what missionaries had to do to receive denominational support, views of the Bible, doctrines about the virgin birth and the second coming of Christ, different perspectives on the historic role of Calvinism, and conflict between premillennialists and postmillennialists. Official splits resulting from the controversy between fundamentalists and liberals included the founding of the Orthodox Presbyterian Church in 1936 and the Bible Presbyterian Church in 1937. Only among Northern Baptists were the battles waged by the fundamentalists as intense.

The Presbyterians' legacy of conflict, however, needs to be understood in perspective. Despite the denomination's early cleavages in the nineteenth century and its involvement in the fundamentalist-modernist controversy, it has not been any more prone to schisms in the twentieth century than the other large denominational families. This at least is the tentative conclusion that has emerged from research on schisms that I have been engaged in with Professors Robert Liebman and John Sutton. We have analyzed data on 175 denominations, including 55 Baptist denominations, 50 Lutheran denominations, 34 Methodist denominations, and 36 Presbyterian and Reformed denominations, between 1890 and 1980. Among these denominations, there were 55 schisms (which we analyzed using a variant of instantaneous hazard models known as event history analysis).

Presbyterians actually had somewhat *higher* probabilities of survival—i.e., *lower* probabilities of schism—than did Methodists, Baptists, or Lutherans. The differences, however, were not statistically significant. We also performed two other tests that bear on the question of whether Presbyterians have been more prone to schisms over the past century than other denominational families. We controlled for any residual effects of denominational family when we examined the effects of other factors that predicted the likelihood of schisms occurring. When we did so, denominational family produced no significant effects. We also examined the effects of church polity type, a variable we coded separately to be able to compare the rate of schisms among denominations with congregational, presbyterian, or episcopal forms of church government. Again, we found no significant differences.[3]

There is, however, one sense in which the Presbyterian family provides an unusually good opportunity for examining the growing cleavage between religious liberals and religious conservatives and other tensions that have surfaced in American religion in recent years. For some years, the denomination has been in the forefront of efforts by denominational agencies themselves to collect systematic data on the beliefs and attitudes of its laity and clergy. Large numbers of questions have been directed over the past decade and a half to random samples of laity and clergy included in the "Presbyterian Panel." Several books and numerous articles have been published from these data. In addition, it is possible to flesh out the nature of changes among Presbyterians through their many denominational reports, annual minutes, and monthly publications.

The Declining Significance of Presbyterianism

The first conclusion that emerges clearly from all this evidence is that Prebyterianism has experienced a serious decline during the past three decades. The decline in membership has, of course, been much commented upon. But there is another kind of decline that may be even more indicative of the changes facing established religious bodies in our society. This is the decline of *denominationalism*. By all indications, Presbyterians have not only been diminishing in numbers but have also experienced an erosion in the social and cultural boundaries that have set them off from other denominations in the past. It will come as no surprise to many within the denomination that this has happened. But it may still be instructive to understand more specifically the ways in which it has happened.

First, some of the social characteristics that used to set Presbyterians off from the rest of the American population have diminished at least marginally in importance. For example, in 1960 Presbyterians were 1.8 times more likely than average to be employed in professional or managerial occupations, but by 1976 they were only 1.4 times more likely to be employed in these occupations.[4] Similarly, in 1956 Presbyterians had been 1.9 times as likely to have attained some college education than was true in the nation as a whole. By 1980, this factor had been reduced to 1.6 times the national average.[5] Over the same period, even more dramatic changes took place in the social characteristics of other denominations. Consequently, in the 1980s Roman Catholics, Baptists, and Lutherans, and even members of fundamentalist sects all resembled Presbyterians more closely on basic social characteristics than they did in the 1950s or 1960s.

Perhaps because of these convergences, Presbyterians as a group also do not differ markedly from the members of other denominations on some of the most salient social and political issues of our time. For instance, attitudes toward abortion have been particularly divisive in the political arena since the Supreme Court's ruling in *Roe v. Wade* in 1973; and yet, on a standard survey question during this period that asked persons whether they approved of abortion for someone who simply did not want more children, the percentages answering yes ranged only between 44 percent among Lutherans, Catholics, and members of Protestant sects and 50 percent among Episcopalians. Baptists, Methodists, Presbyterians, and Jews all scored about midway between these two figures.[6]

Second, much evidence suggests that more Presbyterians mingle with, marry the members of, and switch to other denominations now than ever before. Data collected in the 1970s and early 1980s, for example, showed that 45 percent of all Americans who had been raised as Presbyterians now belonged to some other denomination or to no de-

nomination at all.[7] Interdenominational marriages also
point to a weakening of denominational boundaries. Specifically, a comparison of data from the mid-1970s and the
mid-1950s shows that the percentage of married people
with spouses belonging to the same religion as themselves
declined by 25 percentage points among Presbyterians
over this period.[8]

Third, all of this takes place within a more general climate of theological and cultural tolerance. In the 1940s and
1950s, deep misgivings still separated the members of many
Protestant denominations and, particularly, separated Protestants from Roman Catholics. A Presbyterian pastor, for
example, wrote in an article warning Protestant youth
against marrying Catholics that: "It is Protestant theology,
not Roman Catholic, which has provoked men to demand
free government and the overthrow of tyrants." "It is," he
argued, "Protestant church polity, and not Roman Catholic,
which schools men in the actual practice of democracy."[9] A
few years later the Presbyterian Church U.S.A. adopted a
statement at its annual convention that condemned the
"cultic worship of Mary" among Catholics. Since the Second Vatican Council, such expressions of anti-Catholicism
by Presbyterian leaders have, to say the least, become un-
fashionable and, for the most part, unspeakable.

And finally, the erosion of denominational barriers has
been legitimated by theological and ecclesiastical pronouncements by the denomination itself. The ecumenical
movement has played an important role in fostering
greater cooperation between Presbyterians and other denominations. The denomination has also enacted legislation specifically aimed at lowering denominational
barriers and making it easier for clergy and laity alike to
cross these boundaries. The Confession of 1967 denied
that belief in any particular confession could be held as a
standard of membership or a criterion of belief. It has also
become easier for clergy trained in seminaries outside the
denomination to be ordained. An estimated third of all
Presbyterian clergy, for example, no longer receive training in the denomination's seminaries.

Social Forces and the Denomination's Response

Like other denominational families, Presbyterianism has been exposed on every side to the serious changes taking place in American society since World War II. In the 1950s, its membership grew as the population itself grew. Young families moved to the suburbs, earned good salaries, and took their children to church. Much of the fundamentalism that had dogged the denomination's flanks in the 1930s was now isolated in the smaller Presbyterian sects, and neo-orthodoxy was heard loudly in the denomination's major seminaries. Church leaders called for a moderate blend of personal salvation, evangelism, missionary effort, and social outreach.

In the 1960s, Presbyterians soon became caught up in the larger turmoil of the society. Formal resolutions against racial discrimination gradually gave way to more activist involvement in the civil rights movement. Crises in the cities became the subject of commission reports. And by the end of the decade, campus protests, Black militance, and the Vietnam war were all matters to which church leaders were giving serious attention.

Studies of Presbyterians and other mainstream Protestant denominations in the 1960s and early 1970s suggested that clergy had moved to the "left," which meant championing social justice and minority causes, far more rapidly than the typical parishioner. There was, however, a substantial shift taking place among laity during this period as well—a shift that gave left-leaning clergy more grassroots support as time went on. This was the rapid upgrading in educational levels that the federal government began to sponsor in the 1960s.

Unless one was an Episcopalian, having been to college was rare among the members of all denominations in the 1950s. Fewer than one Baptist, Lutheran, or Catholic in seven had ever been to college; and even among Presbyterians the proportion was only one in three. By the early 1980s, six Presbyterians in ten had been to college.

This change was associated with a number of important

consequences. As young people went through the nation's colleges in the 1960s and 1970s, many swelled the ranks of Presbyterian campus ministries, often providing foot soldiers for the social and political activities of these ministries. Other young people left the church, finding it too staid and traditional, especially in comparison with the dynamism of political movements, communes, and new religious imports from East Asia. The geographic and social mobility, and greater levels of tolerance associated with higher education, increased the likelihood that young Presbyterians would marry outside their own faith, move away from parent congregations, and leave the denomination entirely. The quest for higher education forced young people to postpone marriage and child rearing, resulting in some of the numerical decline the denomination has experienced. And the division between those with better educations and those with lower levels of formal training began to reinforce differences between Presbyterians with liberal theological inclinations and Presbyterians with more conservative and evangelical orientations.

Other social changes influenced the organizational structure of American Presbyterianism directly. As I mentioned earlier, our studies of schisms and mergers show no differences between Presbyterians and other denominational families in their propensity to have undergone these organizational changes, at least in the twentieth century. Our research does, however, reveal the extent to which Presbyterians and other denominational families alike have been subject to the effects of broader strains in their environment. Increases in size, such as the growth that occurred in the 1950s, were an important predictor of subsequent schisms. This is not to say that strife develops more easily in good times than in bad. But it does suggest that larger memberships become increasingly difficult to control, other things being equal. Instability in the broader economic environment, especially business failures—a phenomenon that became increasingly evident in the 1960s and 1970s—proved to be associated with higher rates of denominational schisms as well. We also found that prior mergers, of the kind that many major denominations entered into during the 1960s and 1970s, have a positive effect on the likelihood of schisms occurring. And we found a kind of "contagion" effect among schisms themselves: the presence of a few other schisms in the broader environment seems to diminish the likelihood of still other schisms occurring, but large numbers of schisms greatly increase the likelihood of other schisms. This pattern was especially prominent in the 1960s and early 1970s. We also know from examining the accounts of these schisms that theological cleavages were generally an important factor.

The Struggle Between Liberals and Conservatives

As denominational boundaries in general have diminished in influence, a new division has risen in importance. At the national level, much evidence suggests that this division can best be characterized simply as a division between self-styled religious liberals and religious conservatives. According to national studies, the population divides itself almost evenly between these two categories, with various gradations of extremity and moderation in each. Each of the major religious groupings for which large enough numbers can be obtained also seems to reflect this division. Lutherans, Baptists, Methodists, and Roman Catholics all have about equal numbers of religious liberals and religious conservatives among their members. Evidence also points toward considerable animosity and misgiving on the part of each faction toward the other. Perhaps correctly, religious liberals view their evangelical counterparts as narrow-minded dogmatists, and evangelicals suspect religious liberals of having become doctrinally and morally permissive, if not outright secular.[10]

Some time ago, a book by Dean Hoge, fittingly titled *Division in the Protestant House,* pointed to the presence of a cleavage of much the same kind among Presbyterians. Hoge's research, based on data from Presbyterian clergy and laity in the early 1970s, showed that those who emphasized personal evangelism were deeply divided from those

who emphasized social action. Not only did the two factions have widely differing views of what the church should
be doing, but they differed fundamentally from one another
on theological issues and in social backgrounds as well. Although there was among clergy at least a neo-orthodox
group that occupied middle ground, theological liberals
constituted a clearly identified group at one end of the spectrum, and theological conservatives constituted another
self-identified group at the other end of the spectrum, and
the two groups assigned very different priorities to the various activities and ministries of the church.[11]

In more recent years, harsh words of the kind one might
expect to hear Democrats and Republicans leveling at one
another have fanned the flames of tension between Presbyterian liberals and Presbyterian conservatives. At the 1988
meeting of the General Assembly, for example, an elder
from the Pittsburgh Presbytery succeeded in getting disci-
plinary action taken against the conservative Presbyterian
Lay Committee by charging it with invading the privacy of
her congregation's members. The Committee, she alleged,
was led by "unscrupulous people" whose access to church
membership lists could "enable them to defraud, harass or
even terrorize the people in a congregation."[12] Equally
harsh words about Presbyterian liberals can be found rou-
tinely expressed in conservative publications like *The Presbyterian Layman.*

Studies conducted by the denomination show the extent
to which Presbyterians are currently divided over a number
of issues that have become salient as matters of church policy. One study, for example, showed that about four members in ten believe the denomination should work to
pressure the government of South Africa to end apartheid,
while about three in ten were opposed to this kind of activity.[13] Gender, feminism, and the ordination of women are
other topics that have produced much division of opinion.
Ordination, it appears, has begun to evoke fairly wide-
spread consensus, although half of all members still fear
that appointing a woman in their own congregation would
create strife.[14] But the question of the roles of women more

generally remains a matter over which Presbyterians are divided. One study, for example, found that three members in ten thought "women should worry less about their rights and more about becoming good wives and mothers," while four in ten disagreed.[15]

As in most other denominations and faith traditions, abortion has been a particularly divisive issue. According to national surveys, Presbyterians divide almost evenly between opponents of abortion and those who feel abortion should be a matter of individual choice. Depending on how the question is asked, the proportions who express tolerant views toward abortion range from 47 percent to 56 percent.[16] Not only are Presbyterians divided in their views, each side has also mobilized itself to press its views at governing meetings of the denomination and to the membership at large. Presbyterians Pro-Life, for example, has pressed its ideas actively at both the congregational and national levels, most recently drawing a large crowd at the 1988 General Assembly to hear an impassioned plea for the unborn by its invited speaker, Mother Teresa.

From national surveys, evidence can also be pieced together that shows the extent to which Presbyterians are divided on political orientations. The ratio of self-identified political liberals to self-identified political conservatives, for example, is almost at parity: about a third of all Presbyterians polled between the mid-1970s and early 1980s identified themselves as conservatives, about a third identified themselves as liberals, and the remaining third took a middle-of-the-road position.[17]

These divisions in attitudes and theological identification have been reinforced by a new kind of organization within the denomination: the special purpose group. Although some of these groups—missionary societies, youth organizations, women's groups—have a long history among Presbyterians, their overall numbers have increased noticeably since the 1960s and their character has changed as well. Their impetus, in fact, appears to have been closely linked with the more general turmoil in American society during the 1960s.

In anticipation of the confessional revision in 1967, two special purpose groups were formed by leaders opposed to this revision, and these movements soon gained national followings. One was the Presbyterian Lay Committee, which also played a prominent role in opposing the denomination's protest activities during the Vietnam war; the other was called Presbyterians United for Biblical Concerns. Both have disseminated literature, organized petition campaigns, and lobbied at meetings of the denomination's General Assembly to uphold conservative views of the Bible, as well as to defend doctrines rooted in the Reformation tradition and strict concepts of moral and spiritual discipline.

Other special purpose groups include Presbyterians for Democracy and Religious Freedom, Presbyterians Pro-Life, Presbyterians for Lesbian and Gay Concerns, the Witherspoon Society, the Black Presbyterian Caucus, Presbyterians for Biblical Sexuality, and the Religious Coalition on Abortion Rights. Like political action committees and lobbyist organizations in Washington, these special purpose groups have arisen within the denomination to mobilize grassroots support for particular issues and make this support heard in the denomination's policy-making circles. They function within guidelines established by the denomination. But they clearly add a new layer of organization to the more established hierarchy of authority that has traditionally risen from the ranks of local elders and pastors through regional presbyteries and synods to the General Assembly.

Special purpose groups, moreover, are not simply the work of like-minded individuals who wish to band together for more intimate fellowship or a stronger sense of community. They vary in purpose, and some do have community as their chief objective. But the majority resemble what sociologists have called "struggle groups": that is, special interests organized specifically to engage in combat with other special interests, to champion their own cause, and to see their cause win over the hearts and minds of denominational officials. In the words of a recent editorial in the newspaper of one such pressure group, "the church will be changed by a proliferation of sharply focused, single-issue groups, each of which is willing to get down in the trenches and fight."[18]

And yet, despite the fact that these pressure groups are devoted to single issues, there has also been a notable tendency for them to stack up into two opposing camps, one championing conservative issues of all kinds, the other adopting liberal positions across the board. Thus, a group like the Presbyterian Lay Committee not only struggles to "put greater emphasis on the teaching of the Bible as the authoritative Word of God," as its official objective states, but also provides a sympathetic forum for everything from anti-gay activists, to opponents of a nuclear freeze, to apologists for big companies engaged in lucrative business with South Africa.

Divisions at the Congregational Level

What impact have these conflicts between liberals and conservatives had at the congregational level? Here our evidence is sparse, but we do have some clues both from aggregate studies and from case histories of particular congregations. At the aggregate level, we know from Gallup data that religious liberals and religious conservatives report having contact with members of the opposing faction in their local churches and even in Bible study groups and prayer fellowships. Although the numbers are small, this was true among Presbyterians just as it was in the sample as a whole.

The Gallup data also show that individuals who had made contact with the opposing faction in these local settings were almost as likely to hold negative views of their opponents as were those whose contact had come in less personal settings. Among those who identified themselves as religious liberals, 42 percent whose contact with conservatives had been in their current church held negative opinions of conservatives. Roughly the same proportions harbored negative sentiments when their contact had been

in a Bible study group or prayer fellowship. The only type
of contacts that were associated with significantly higher
levels of negative sentiment were contact in a former
church and exposure to conservatives from reading or television. Similar patterns were evident among persons who
identified themselves as conservatives.[19]

A more detailed glimpse at the dynamics of conflict in
local congregations is available in R. Stephen Warner's
valuable study of a Presbyterian church in Mendocino,
California. Warner observed a congregation caught in the
throes of a theological transition. Its character was vastly
different at the end of the 1970s from what it had been in
the late 1960s. As it turns out, I had made a pilgrimage to
this church myself in 1970. My impression, which Warner's retrospective research confirmed, was that the church
sheltered a kind of bland milquetoast liberalism that
seemed to be all too common among small Presbyterian
congregations in California in those days. A decade later it
had become a vibrant home of evangelical fervor. The
change was relatively abrupt and involved some unusual
circumstances in the surrounding community. Evangelicalism triumphed, but not without difficulty. It triumphed by
converting some, by bringing in new members, and above
all, by capturing the seat of power within the congregation
and using it to bring in new leadership favorable to its
cause. The new spirit was scarcely an evangelicalism of the
radical right. And yet the liberal constituency found its
worldview so much at odds with the new leadership that
many found it impossible to stay in the congregation at
all.[20]

In somewhat less dramatic fashion, but I suspect in a
more typical way, the conflicts Warner observed were also
evident in a church in New Jersey that I watched as both
participant and observer between the mid-1970s and the
mid-1980s. This was an independent community church, a
grandchild, as it were, of Presbyterianism, whose own history provided an interesting commentary on the denomination. It was pastored by a minister whose training and
sympathies lay in the Presbyterian tradition, both theolog-

ically and in matters of church government. His grandfather had been the pastor of a leading Presbyterian church in New York City. His father, too, had been a Presbyterian minister but had left the denomination in the 1950s, distraught by the liberal tendencies he saw developing, and started an independent church with the help of others sharing his concerns. His son's church was also independent, not so much in protest against Presbyterianism, but because its founders simply saw pragmatic advantages in remaining independent.

When I first came into contact with the congregation in the mid-1970s, shortly after its founding as a branch church in a new suburban community, it showed all the signs of having found a happy way of accommodating parishioners from both the right and the left. The theological center of gravity was perhaps slightly to the right of Presbyterian churches in the area. But it was administered by a Presbyterian-style board of elders, accommodated people with differing views of the sacraments, and combined solid preaching with a strong commitment to fellowship, outreach, and service to the community. Leaders in the congregation varied in their personal views from strong supporters of the American Civil Liberties Union and the nuclear freeze movement to militant anti-Communists.

Over the next decade, I witnessed this unity-amid-diversity unravel. The congregation experienced in microcosm what was happening to the structure of American religion at large. Indeed, the pressures from without—the impact of the nation's public religion—often contributed to the growing strife within. At first, during the Carter years, it was the increasing popularity of the evangelical movement nationally that began to shape the congregation's policies: pressures for the pastor to align himself with the National Association of Evangelicals, increasing emphasis on church growth, speakers and tapes that reflected the subculture of American evangelicalism. Then, for a time, it was the left who, without consciously thinking of themselves as an alternative force, pushed the congregation to adopt its causes and orientations: upgrading the church's preaching and educational programs to better appeal to the surrounding intellectual and professional substratum of the community, publicly supporting the nuclear freeze, finding ways to bring racial diversity to the church, becoming involved in the Nestlé boycott and starting a food cooperative, and eventually rethinking the church's position on gender and the role of women in leadership positions. At the same time, a countertendency began to appear on the right. With the intellectual and professional strata of the community remaining for the most part unchurched, the congregation grew primarily from the ranks of the working class, older people, migrants from the Midwest and South, and professionals with little exposure to the liberal arts, especially business managers and engineers. Demands for basic Bible study rose from their ranks. Discussions of Jerry Falwell and other television preachers became more common. A local pregnancy clinic the church had supported began pressuring members to become politically active in the pro-life movement. Those who had pressed for gender equality were labeled "liberals" and "feminists." Increasingly, the congregation moved to the right, even to the point of refusing to participate in community services with churches whose denominations belonged to the National Council of Churches.

Today, the church remains the victim of the struggles it experienced in the early 1980s. Three ministers have come and gone. Many of the active members have gravitated either to churches more clearly to the right or to mainline churches more tolerant of diversity. Plans for a new building to accommodate an expected membership of a thousand have been postponed indefinitely. And while new housing developments spring up all around it, the remaining congregation of two hundred members struggles to pay its debts and keep its parking lot free of weeds.

Some, of course, have begun to argue that the tension between religious liberals and religious conservatives is now largely a thing of the past at the congregational level. Conflict is receding, they suggest, because conservatism is on the verge of triumph. Both the cases just cited suggest this may be the case, and anecdotal evidence provides ample support for this conclusion. In many congregations, Bible study groups can be found that did not exist a decade ago. More emphasis is evident on Christian education for children and adults alike. Prayer fellowships have sprung up. Aggressively experimental forms of worship have been replaced by more conventional formats. And conservative laity have curbed the ambitions of their more liberal-minded pastors and fellow laity, often resulting in retreats from such issues as gay rights, pro-choice movements, and the nuclear freeze.

How representative such anecdotal accounts may be is difficult to gauge. Certainly the newspapers and rumor mills feed more on examples of new trends than on examples of old patterns simply repeating themselves. However, some evidence from research studies points to the same conclusion. Particularly telling were the results of a survey conducted in 1987 among one thousand randomly selected Presbyterian congregations (of which 610 eventually returned questionnaires). When asked about the theological composition of their congregations, a majority of the elders surveyed said their congregations were moderately conservative.[21]

If we assume for the moment that the dominant tendency at the congregational level is in fact to the right, we then need to decipher some of the reasons why this trend may be taking place, and on that basis come to a better understanding of how it may connect to the broader, more public contours of religion in American society. One possibility that seems to have some empirical support is that elders themselves constitute a conservative force in local congregations. This is not to say that elders are any more conservative than pastors or other members in their social, political, or theological attitudes. Or if they are, their conservatism is at least selective.[22] Elders do, however, seem to worry more about how other parishioners will respond to change, and are somewhat less likely to want to risk initiating change. For example, a *Presbyterian Panel* survey found that elders were significantly more likely than pastors to predict a decline in church participation in their congregations if a woman were called as pastor. The study also showed that elders were less likely than pastors to say they would try to convince the congregation that a woman should be called, and more likely than pastors to say they would either take a neutral position or withdraw the woman's name and recommend a man.[23] Thus, whether it reflects their own disposition or simply their views of what is best for the congregation, elders may actually be one of the active factors moving local congregations toward a more conservative posture.

Other tendencies—ones we can infer from broader studies of religious commitment in American life—also point toward a strengthening of the conservative orientation. One is that much of the fervor of the 1960s and 1970s, the fervor of social activism and experimentation that figured in the liberalism of the period, has been displaced by narrower, more materialistic concerns, and the political climate of the nation has shifted considerably toward a platform of strong defenses, nostalgia for the past, individualism, family, and traditional morality. Another is that rising levels of education appear to be associated not only with more liberal views on many theological questions but also with defection from organized religion entirely. Consequently, the numerical increases in college-educated persons in America do not necessarily translate into active, committed leadership with liberal orientations in the churches. Furthermore, theological liberalism has, by its very nature, championed diversity and the sanctity of alternative quests for the divine in a way that sometimes undercuts strong appeals to stay loyal to the local church and become a booster of its programs.

There are, however, two tendencies that help replenish the liberal wing of the Presbyterian Church. One is the role of women. My research suggests that in most denominations women with college educations are only modestly more likely to be active in their churches than women in the same denominations without college educations, and when college-educated women hold feminist views, their church participation is considerably lower. This pattern is not the case among Presbyterian women, though. Presbyterian women with at least some college education are twice as likely to attend church regularly as Presbyterian women with no college training (the proportions are 50 percent and 25 percent, respectively).[24] The data also show that Presbyterian women who gave feminist responses to attitude questions were no less likely to attend church regularly than were Presbyterian women who gave more traditional responses.[25] If these results are valid, they suggest that women with more education and with sympathy to the feminist movement—that is, women most likely to share sympathies with liberal views on other social and religious issues—are likely to remain active in the church. Moreover, the numbers of these women may actually increase as more and more women attain higher education and adopt gender-egalitarian values.

It is also instructive to speculate about why this pattern holds in the Presbyterian Church and not in most other denominations. Two characteristics of Presbyterian women stand out. A relatively high proportion overall do have at least some college training (in these data, 42 percent did, compared with an average of only 25 percent for all Protestant women). And a relatively high proportion hold gender-egalitarian values (58 percent compared with 42 percent among Protestant women as a whole). In short, Presbyterian women with these characteristics are likely to feel they have kindred spirits in their congregations and, for this reason, may feel more comfortable remaining active in these congregations. This interpretation is, incidentally, supported by patterns evident in the two other traditions—Episcopal and Jewish—in which better-educated women with feminist orientations constitute a significant share of the population. Among Episcopal and Jewish women, higher levels of education and feminist orientations were positively associated with religious involvement.

The other social characteristic that augurs well for the liberal wing of Presbyterianism is the fact that denominational switching follows, to some extent, educational distinctions. Several examples will illustrate. If we look at persons in national surveys who were raised in Baptist churches but are no longer members of Baptist churches, about ten percent of those who have been to college switch to Presbyterian churches, while the figure among those who have not been to college is only five percent. Similarly, if we look at former Methodists, 11 percent of the college-educated group have become Presbyterians, while only 6 percent of the non-college group have. And among persons who formerly belonged to Protestant sects, 15 percent of those with college educations have become Presbyterians, while only 5 percent of those without college educations have become Presbyterians. In other words, the Presbyterian church draws better educated members who leave other denominations more than it does less educated persons. And, generally speaking, higher levels of education are strongly associated with more liberal theological, social, and political views. Thus, it seems reasonable to infer that the Presbyterian Church is gaining some members from other denominations who are switching from a more conservative environment to one in which they can feel more comfortable.[26]

Prospects for Reconciliation

Although there may be some possibility that the division between Presbyterian liberals and Presbyterian conservatives will be healed simply by the triumph of the latter, I believe the evidence on the whole points more toward a continuation of this division. It is, of course, rooted to some extent in reactions to policies of the denomination and with the secular arena. Major shifts in these policies, say, a Supreme Court decision reversing *Roe v. Wade,* or a major war in Central America, could alter the terms of discussion considerably. But the strife between Presbyterian liberals and conservatives has deeper roots than concerns about these specific issues. It reflects broader currents in the society; the mass media fan the flames of contention whenever a new scandal erupts among religious broadcasters; political candidates and right-wing special purpose groups find it is to their advantage to levy direct-mail campaigns at religious audiences; and within Presbyterianism itself, too many special purpose groups have become organized to let controversy simply fade from view.

The cleavage between liberal and conservative Presbyterians is, in my view, both serious and unfortunate. Although it may, at its best, ensure that different points of view are heard in denominational bureaucracies, it has become a means to an end that often overshadows the end itself. Certainly the biblical image of love, or more modern ideals of community and reconciliation, are difficult to see amid the turmoil that divides liberals and conservatives.

This division should not, however, be blamed for the numerical problems Presbyterians have been facing over the past two decades. To the contrary, the mobilization of conservatives at least has probably checked some of the numerical drift the denomination has experienced. And other factors, including increases in average age, lower birth rates, higher levels of education, more and more women entering the labor market, and the location of local churches in declining neighborhoods, probably account for this drift more effectively than does the contention between liberals and conservatives.

At the same time, the numerical losses of the denomination should not, in my view, become an excuse for each side attempting to impute blame to the other side and engaging in activities that damn the enemy within. In a shrinking religious market, acrimony of this kind is all too easy to give vent to. Conservatives can make their voice louder if they proclaim declining numbers to be the result of gay clergy, the murderous immorality of pro-choice activists, unreasonable criticisms of wealthy contributors to the church, and a wishy-washy stand on biblical authority. Liberals can gain temporary satisfaction by convincing themselves that conservative denominations are waging a conspiratorial war against the Presbyterian Church to steal

its members. But neither kind of allegation has been sub-
stantiated with solid empirical evidence. And even if it
were, a war to the bitter end is not only likely to drain the
denomination's resources even more; it also runs contrary
to the doctrines of love and reconciliation that lie at the
core of Christianity.

2

The Presbyterian Heritage
as Modernism:
Reaffirming a Forgotten Past
in Hard Times

Edward W. Farley

In colonial times American religion meant the Episcopalians, the Congregationalists, and the Presbyterians, the big three.[1] Today, there are more Roman Catholics in America than all three combined, more Muslims than Episcopalians, more people who identify themselves by the Hindu method of transcendental meditation than Presbyterians. American religion now has, as Martin Marty says, a new map.[2] And what is mapped is a massive realignment of American religious demography. A vast earthquake has shifted the so-called mainline denominations from the center to the margin of American religious life, a marginality not just of numbers but of vitality and influence.[3] Occupying the new center are large, rapidly growing, aggressive, politically and religiously conservative Protestant denominations. The story of the shift begins a long time ago and includes the creation of the American melting pot from waves of European migrations that added new populations to English New England and the Spanish West, the arrival of a large population of Black slaves, recent new populations of Latins and Asians, and a low birthrate and low natural growth of the mainline denominations.[4] The effects of the earthquake seem long-term. No one expects a shift back to the way things used to be.

Life on the Ecclesiastical Margin

The marginalization of mainline Protestantism is not a secret, something known only by a few statisticians and historians. We all experience it in some way. We experience it when we see the major communication instrument of our day, television, utterly dominated by fundamentalist religious entrepreneurs; when we drive through the small towns and see the Presbyterian church with its 75 members and its hundred-year-old church and five new and very large edifices built by Nazarenes, Southern Baptists, and Churches of Christ; when we realize that our national Presidents and candidates for President can be Roman Catholic, Southern Baptist, Black Baptist, and even Greek Orthodox; when we are no longer surprised to find huge religiously conservative bookstores in our large shopping centers or to learn that conservative seminaries count students by the thousands instead of the low hundreds. We could go on. The earthquake, that is, the displacement and decline of mainline Protestantism, is now a fact of life. This fact is not just the realization that there are many religious traditions different from our own. It is the experience of a loss of national or local visibility and influence, an experience of being on the fringe and on the slope of decline in numbers and vitality.[5]

The experience includes our own response to life on the fringe and on the slope. How are we responding to the earthquake?[6] Well, we have instigated a number of important statistical, historical, and sociological studies with more to come. We have thought up various programs with catchy titles that sound like ad agency commercials: Celebrate, New Age Dawning. We have written some confessional statements, three in 25 years. And we have become very self-preoccupied. We are more worried about whether our candidates for the ministry go to our own seminaries. We try to persuade ourselves that we are not evangelistic enough. We talk much more about "the Reformed tradition." (This very essay indicates such self-preoccupation.) But, for the most part, we do not know what to do. We cannot wave a magic wand and increase our birthrate, or turn the clock back so as to cancel the American melting pot. We would not even want to return America back to the big three or to some sort of established national religion that would stem the tide of secularism.

It should not be necessary to say that the earthquake, the displacement and decline of mainline Protestantism, is an occasion of great temptation. Communities are like individual human beings in that times of decline, uncertainty, insecurity, and threat are times of greatest temptation. When threatened with harm, extinction, or even change, we human beings will latch on to all sorts of ideologies, worldviews, demagogues, authorities, and institutions that we think may save us. Times of peril and insecurity are times of idolatries and absolutisms. After the earthquake, things we thought we had outgrown begin to look attractive again: a new, narrower denominationalism, provincialism, and nostalgia, even schemes of the old dogmatics. After the earthquake, we begin to envy religious movements that glitter with power and slick success and wonder whether to imitate them. After the earthquake, we look for aspects of our heritage we might blame for our failures—our ecumenism, our commitment to scholarship, our social witness. In the face of these temptations, I want to try to make a case for another response, a kind of calling we may have in the situation of displacement and decline, a calling to recover and more vigorously pursue a certain part of our heritage.

Secular and Critical Modernism

Since a religious community is as corruptible as any other human community, its past and its heritage may be as much a burden and shame as a glory to be celebrated. We Presbyterians do not escape the truth of Jesus' parable; our historical existence is a mixture of wheat and tares.

There are things to be celebrated in our liturgical, moral, and theological tradition; a tradition founded by Calvin and Zwingli, honed by seventeenth-century European school theologies, narrowed by the Swiss school and broadened and modified by the French school of Saumur, the federal theologies of Holland, and by English puritanism. In a time of uncertainty and peril and of the ascendancy of conservative Protestantism, we are prone to see that tradition as a kind of preserve that needs maintaining, a deposit of doctrines that need recollecting.

But deposits of doctrines are not the genius of this tradition. Most of the doctrines of the Presbyterian heritage we share with Lutherans and Christendom at large, and most Presbyterians do not even know the specific controversies that set the rather subtle doctrinal differences between the Reformed churches and their opponents. If we did know them, we would probably regard them as passé. If we have a genius or "way" as John Mackay calls it, it is not so much some distinctive deposit of doctrine as a way of transcending our deposited traditions under the constant nagging pressure of the question of truth. Mackay argued that the Presbyterian way was a passion for truth and objectivity that opposed all equating of human expressions of "the truth as it is in Jesus with the truth itself."[7] John Leith speaks of the historical genius of Presbyterianism (which he thinks is seriously endangered) to be a concern with the *content* and the life of the mind. And Brian Gerrish describes those in the Reformed tradition who "claimed the right to a critical use of tradition," as "in principle claiming nothing more than did Luther and Calvin."[8] In other words, the genius of the Presbyterian heritage is its *critical modernism.*

Why describe this genius by the term "modernism"? I am using the term in a descriptive and not just metaphorical sense. I must admit that even used descriptively, modernism is an ambiguous term. First, it is ambiguous as a historical term since it describes quite different movements of recent religious history. Initially, it named a turn-of-the-century Roman Catholic movement condemned by

Pius X. In Protestant history it is used in two ways, first, as a label for the extremely liberal wing of liberal Protestantism, in which case a distinction is posited between evangelical liberals like Charles A. Briggs and William Adams Brown and modernists like Shailer Mathews and Gerald Birney Smith. Second, it is also the term used in the 1920s for the theological alternative to fundamentalism.[9]

As a theological category, modernism contains a deeper ambiguity. On the one hand, it describes the tendency to displace the distinctive witness of the gospel with secular or cultural contents. In this sense the translation of Christian faith into categories of pop psychology or the translation of theological symbols into the categories of a philosophical system are modernisms. Let us call this usage *secular* or *cultural modernism.*[10] On the other hand, modernism names an openness to the various discoveries, sciences, and criteria that have arisen with modernity and to the task of making positive use of these in the interpretation and understanding of the Christian gospel. This is the modernism that evoked the theological battles of the nineteenth and early twentieth centuries and that posed the issues of the modernist-fundamentalist controversies over biblical criticism, selected doctrines, and evolution. Let us call this *critical modernism.*

Christianity as a type of religious faith is especially open to both cultural and critical modernism because its conviction that no specific cultural form, nation, ethnicity, or gender is necessary to salvation prompts it to appropriate a great variety of cultural forms and worldviews. The history of the Christian church and its theology is thus a history of continual new appropriations of culture: Roman *auctoritas* and law into church structures; the ancient goddess tradition into Mariology; Platonism into theology; Victorian manners and customs into piety. And the appropriations of culture continue. Virtually all contemporary American religions from the Protestant mainline to the *nouveau riche* conservative churches have elements of secular modernism. The therapeutic mind-set seems to dominate the mainline churches but is also very much present in the conservative churches.[11] The functionalist rationality of technological and media religion and of professionalism is especially manifest in the conservative churches but is present in tamed form in the mainline churches. Contemporary Presbyterianism is modernist in both senses. Its secular modernism shows up in therapeutic, managerial, and professionalist shapings of its congregations, bureaucracies, and seminaries, but in an arrested form. Compared to Robert Schuller, Presbyterian therapeutic and professionalism is very much tamed. And *critical* modernism has so deeply shaped Presbyterianism that the matters modernists fought for in the 1920s are now simply taken for granted. I want to focus now on the critical modernism of the Presbyterian heritage, and I want to argue that if we Presbyterians want to have a guilty conscience, it should be about the tacit, hidden secular modernism eating away at our vitals; and if we have a calling, it should be to continue and sharpen our critical modernism.

Critical Modernism in the Deep Structures of Presbyterianism

A quick study of the history of Presbyterianism in America shows what seems to be the opposite of a community inclined to modernism. From colonial times to well into the twentieth century, the Presbyterian Church appears to be a very conservative, tradition-oriented community, successfully resisting all attempts at confessional change, hunting down heretics whenever they appear, and even introducing subscriptionist vows for ordination to protect its doctrinal deposit.[12] But let us see how we react to the following issues.

> Do you subscribe to the five points of Calvinism as articulated by the Synod of Dort or to all the affirmations of the Westminster Confession?
> Do you see the Westminster Confession as such an absolutely adequate expression of the gospel for all places, peoples, contexts, and future times that it should never be revised, amended, or added to?

Do you think that historical methods are appropriate and useful in studying the Bible, determining who wrote its texts, its layers of traditions, the situations these layers reflect?

Do you approach the Bible on the assumption of literal inerrancy of every specific text so that the geology, dates, historical descriptions, and biology of those texts are guaranteed to be accurate and true for all time?

Do you reject the discoveries, methods, and advances of modern geology, biology, genetics, and astronomy, including the evolutionary account of the biological history of species?

Do you reject the social character of the Christian gospel, the sense in which it has to do with the transformation of corporate evil, systems of oppression, because you see its terminating point in the creation of individual virtues and the salvation of the individual soul?

Do you reject other branches of Christendom and denominations as simply false or highly suspect versions of the gospel under the conviction that there is one true version of Christianity, the Reformed and Presbyterian tradition?

My guess is that most of us, including most Presbyterians, answered no to these questions. I further suspect that most answered no with an accompanying yawn, because these are not the issues we find ourselves agonizing over, worried lest we be tried for heresy before a church judicatory. At one time, though, most Presbyterians would have answered yes to these questions.

The question is, what happened? Did an angel of the Lord appear to a denomination mired in its own traditionalism and effect an overnight miracle so that Presbyterians all woke up the next day with a different set of convictions? Here we need more than a quick study of Presbyterian history. Six issues stand out in two centuries of struggle in the Presbyterian Church between critical modernism and its opponents. I state them in the form of questions.

1. Is the Calvinist theology and theological system modifiable?

2. Are the confessions and creeds that express our corporate faith relative, fallible, and revisable?

3. Is a thoroughgoing historical approach to the Bible proper, useful, even necessary for its interpretation?

4. Is the gospel, and theological truth, part of and consistent with the larger truth of the world that the sciences, philosophy, and the humanities attempt to discern?

5. Is the Christian church a pluralism of communities that are called to cooperate with and respect each other and even celebrate each other's differences?

6. Is the Christian gospel social in character?

The last two centuries of American Presbyterian history have seen plenty of fireworks. These six issues summarize what those fireworks are about.

Is Reformed theology modifiable?   The question is, of course, rhetorical. Reformed theology was never simply a single fixed system. However, by the eighteenth century a very conservative form of that theology had taken root in colonial America which was subjected to criticism and change by the New England theologians in the line of Jonathan Edwards. This movement that liberalized the Scotch-Irish side of the Presbyterian tradition found expression in the nineteenth century in what was called the New School, and an actual separation of Presbyterians took place for the thirty-two years following 1837. The issue? The truth, coherence, and adequacy of the conservative form of Calvinism. The modifications continued in the form of the New Theology, and while Karl Barth and neo-orthodoxy may seem conservative to some theologians, that movement is a radical modification of Calvinism in its seventeenth century scholastic and puritan expressions. We take the modification of the old Calvinism for granted.

Are Presbyterian confessional statements revisable?   Since the Presbyterian tradition was born amid a protest against a church absolutizing its own creedal and theological tradition, one would expect Presbyterians to have a high sense of the fallibility and revisability of their confessions. But something tends to happen to prophetic movements of protest and to vital religious movements. Because they experience the new power of grace through the work of their founders and since this work is expressed in their confession, they tend to give the same absolute status to these human works as they do to the God who saves. Thus the Presbyterian heritage introduced what had not been there in the beginning, the attempt to assure the gospel's truth by subscriptional vows to specific doctrines, specifically, five doctrines regarded as the essence of Calvinism. And with this came a resistance to altering the Westminister Confession in any respect.

But a countercurrent had been at work since the early nineteenth century. The Presbyterian participation in the revivals during the Great Awakening resulted in what was called the New Side, which was both a more moderate Calvinism and a reaffirmation of experiential religion in the face of an overemphasis on religion's doctrinal and legal aspects. After the Civil War this countercurrent found a clear and decisive voice in a Chicago pastor, David Swing, who said plainly that church confessions were not deposits of absolute truth but statements having a useful function for a specific time and situation in the church's .ife.[13] Pressed by the charges of Francis Patton, Swing was tried and vindicated by Chicago Presbytery. We all know the outcome of the countercurrent, namely, the decision to let a cluster of confessional statements express the church's beliefs, thereby undercutting the absolute authority of any one confession or statement within. And one of those confessions says explicitly: "No one type of confession is exclusively valid, no one statement is irreformable" (C. 1967, Preface). The implication is that the expression of the church's faith should occur in continuing restatements that reflect new knowledge, new situations, new imageries, and new perspectives. Confessions are not absolute and timeless: they are experiential, fallible, utilitarian, and situational.

Is a historical approach to scripture proper and useful?
The formal principle of the Reformation was *sola scrip-*

tura. Scripture alone is the measure of the church's witness. But what is *scriptura?* According to a very ancient and even pre-Christian paradigm, scripture means a collection of texts whose originating inspiration guarantees the truth and accuracy of each specific asserted content. The unit of scripture's truth is, accordingly, the sentence, the exegeted verse. Elements in Renaissance textual scholarship and even in some of the Reformers are at odds with this paradigm. Nevertheless, the paradigm was elaborated into a technical hermeneutic in seventeenth-century Protestant school theology, a heritage transmitted to American Presbyterianism. There was no single refutation of this paradigm, rather a deluge of historical evidences for the human, churchly, and theological character of *scriptura.* Originating in Europe long before, the historical approach to scripture was slow in coming to American Presbyterianism, and when it came its exponents were put on trial, with the result that the church lost both its most gifted biblical scholar of the day, Charles A. Briggs, and its main New School seminary, Union Seminary.[14] But these victories of Old Side and Princetonian Presbyterianism could not hold back the massive tides of linguistic, archaeological, literary, redactional, and other scholarship that simply swept the old paradigm away. Thus the historical approach to scripture has now been taken for granted in the seminaries for forty years or more.

Is the gospel consistent with the larger world of knowledge and the sciences? Another wave, virtually a tidal wave, was approaching the shores of Protestant America, the wave of the new sciences of earth, cosmos, and life. Like the Roman Catholic churches of Galileo's time, the Protestant churches of nineteenth-century America offered an initial resistance. The scientific challenge to biblical cosmology and biology had begun in the sixteenth century, so that in the seventeenth century, the Reverend Thomas Burnet could write a work, *The Sacred Theory of the Earth,* trying to reconcile biblical geology and the new science. In post-Civil War America, the theory of evolution was the test case, dividing such divines as Charles Hodge (against) and James McCosh (for). This too turned into a deluge, not because of scientific consensus about the mechanism of the evolutionary process, or the Darwin-Wallace theory of natural selection or its alternatives, but because of the massive data concerning the antiquity and the continuity of all life forms on our planet. The evolutionists lost the Scopes trial but won the war. With evolutionary biology and other sciences, the church was presented a choice; reject the sciences and their piling up of new evidences, thus placing faith, religion, God, gospel, and church on what appears to be the side of falsehood, reality denial, and even dishonesty, or remain open to the truth wherever it appears and of whatever kind it is. The Presbyterian Church rejected the way of scientific obscurantism and opted for the second alternative.[15]

Is the Christian church a pluralism of communities whose differences call for cooperation and mutual respect? The experience of different and competing forms of religion, and even of Christianity, has been in the Christian movement since the days of the apostle Paul. But the issue of pluralism is not the same as the issue of diversity. A pluralist posture grants legitimacy to the other form of faith and even celebrates its difference. In earlier times the branches and denominations of Christendom were related to each other through controversy, polemics, and competition, a relation which assumes that one's own version of the gospel is the one true version, the one and only authentic instance of obedience and faithfulness. To the degree that a denomination had this posture, it simply competed with other denominations and regarded cooperation and union as disobedient compromises. In the earlier epoch virtually all forms of Christendom retained this posture and Presbyterians were no exception. Guided by this posture, Presbyterians spawned new denominations and underwent splits in their ranks; Old Side and New Side, Old School and New School, North and South.

On the other hand, this history too has a countercurrent,

an uneasy conscience about the denominationalism that prompted the desire to reconcile divided Christendom. One Plan of Union was directed even to the Congregationalists, and while that was voted down, the church has successfully accomplished a number of reunions. From the 1920s on, self-absolutizing and narrow denominationalism was replaced in the Presbyterian Church with an ecumenical spirit that resulted in participation and even leadership in the national and world ecumenical movement and in a mood to reconcile the branches of Presbyterianism and explore union with other denominations.[16]

Is the Christian gospel social in character? Centuries of Christendom have been dominated by the assumption that the deep structures of political, economic, racial, and gender oppressions are not changeable. The gospel gives human beings resources to bear up under those structures and prepares them for the afterlife; it is not addressed to the fallen and unchangeable structures themselves. This posture of an earlier time has also been displaced. Well known is the role the Presbyterian clergy played in colonial times in changing one deep political structure, the shift from colonial monarchy to a democracy, expressing therefore a vision of a certain kind of society and its attainability. But it was especially the social gospel movement of the early twentieth century that pressed the issue of the social character of the gospel. And while its framework was an optimism and progressivism that few people now share, its legacy is at work when the church takes its stand against dehumanizing movements of modern culture, when it confronts racism and sexism within itself and the larger society, when it debates issues of militarism and the pollution of the planet. Rare now is the view that the gospel is simply a message about a trans-earthly destiny of individual souls. Few doubt that the Christian gospel has something to do with systemic evil and our social well-being.

These six spheres are now part of the deep convictions of the Presbyterian Church. They are also what modernism was all about. These were the very issues debated, fought over, in the nineteenth and early twentieth centuries. The outcome was what Lefferts Loetscher called "the broadening church," and the content of this broadening resides in these six convictions. None of these issues is really up for current debate. No presbytery is going to refuse ordination to a candidate who thinks the Westminster Confession is fallible, contextual, and revisable, who thinks the gospel has something to say about racism, sexism, and ecology, or who uses von Rad or Bultmann in the study of the Bible.

When we look closely at these convictions, we realize that they are not just six separate issues but are part of a single woven fabric. For instance, if we think scripture should be studied historically because its texts have a history and are rooted in historical settings and reflect the historical responses of the authors, we surely are also going to think about John Calvin, the Westminster Assembly, the Reformed tradition, and the Presbyterian denomination in the same way. And if we are open to the evidences of historical method, that is going to be part of a larger openness to any and all evidences from any and all sciences.

These convictions then are part of one overall conviction. Expressed negatively, it is the refusal to make anything human and historical a timeless absolute, dwelling above the flow of contexts and situations. One refuses to give this status of the timeless and the unconditional to one's denomination, to one's confessions, to one's Reformed heritage, even to one's scripture. In this negative sense and as a theological position, modernism is a radical prophetism refusing to identify any human entity with God. Expressed positively, it is the conviction that God's presence and truth come through human and historical and fallible vessels. Positively, modernism is the conviction that God redeems, transforms, and empowers in and through the earthen vessels of the creaturely, the cultural, the historical. If we need certainty about salvation, modernism would direct that to God and God alone, not to the vessels that deliver it.

Critical Modernism: Repressions and Ambivalences

All I have said so far is that modernism is in our history
and has become an accepted part of what we are. I want to
conclude with three affirmations. First, critical modernism
is not only part of our recent history but is an expression of
our very old and deep heritage. Second, critical modernism is present in an arrested form today and there is ambivalence about it and even resistance to it. Third, the
heritage of critical modernism sets before us what might be
the calling of the Presbyterian Church in a time of decline.

What does critical modernism have to do with the older
and deeper heritage of Reformed faith? It can be said that
it has nothing to do with it simply because it is a *modernism.* Thus, it can be seen to be an accretion, something
which was not always there and which can be easily dis-
pensed with, a coat we can shed whenever we want, especially when other denominations turn the heat up. There is
something that is a deep part of our heritage: a certain
persistent and trouble-causing concern for truth. Reformed churches fought with Lutherans over the ubiquity
of Christ's ascended body because of a *philosophical* concern. They argued that the idea of an all-present *body* was
philosophically implausible. Something about this heritage
cannot settle for a version of the gospel that is mere non-
sense, that requires the sacrifice of the intellect, that is
anti-intellectual, that assigns faith to the sphere of emotion
only, that reduces truth to functions and to pragmatics. I
am not sure where this came from. Calvin's debates with
his Roman Catholic opponents show a sharp and ruthless
intellectuality which argues what is the case about Christian history and the meaning of texts. Perhaps that set the
tone. Perhaps it is the sense that all of creation is the
sphere of God and God's working and no manifest truth
about that world can be simply dismissed. Whatever the
rootage, when this posture enters the modern world, it cannot turn its back on what is happening. And if evidences
accumulate as to the historical character of the church's
earthen vessels of redemption, it cannot turn its back on

that. This is why I think that critical modernism is not a superficial addition but an expected response in the Presbyterian heritage.

How is critical modernism a part of the present church? I have argued that it is part of our taken-for-granted convictions. I now want to argue that it is present in an arrested form. What does this mean? It means we have not pressed the Calvinist theology and its themes and dominant metaphors hard enough. We are too quick to think that Karl Barth's restatement handles all the problems and is utterly sufficient. A new chorus of voices has raised issues of the nature of revelation, the effect of situations on theology, the hegemony of Western male modes of thought, and many other themes we dare not ignore. And listening to those voices will mean a continuing reinterpretation of our theological tradition. In the writing of new situationally based confessional statements, we have acknowledged the historical and revisable nature of confessions. But the confessions we write tend to stay away from hard theological questions and few state with full conviction and in an unambiguous way the modernist themes we all believe.

An exception is the statement in the Confession of 1967 that "the Scriptures . . . are nevertheless the words of men, conditioned by language, thought forms, and literary fashions of the places and times at which they were written."[17] But this modernist notion of the historical character of the Bible seems to be present in the church more in a whisper than in a loud voice. The result is that the clergy take it for granted and the laity and their church school materials still know little about it. Another result is the persistence of precritical ways of using the Bible in preaching that simply "apply" specific passages of scripture to present situations.

As for the sciences, we may be amused by the creationist issue of the fundamentalists, but for the most part there is a moratorium on the whole issue of what the gospel is in the setting of a world like ours, where human beings and the planet earth cannot be assumed to be the center and

telos of creation, where biologists and physicists both argue for an ultimate randomness in the micro-events that
constitute reality, where virtually everything about individual and social human being has some evolutionary and
genetic background. We have rejected fundamentalist obscurantism only to be content with two utterly separatea
worlds, the world of actual events studied by the sciences,
and the world of faith.

As for postures of ecumenism and pluralism, we nave
acknowledged that other Christian communities can be
vessels of God's salvific working, that there is a place for
this variety of traditions. But we are only on the threshold
of acknowledging that God might be salvifically working
through the communities of other religious faiths, that
Buddhism and Hinduism and Judaism and Native American religions are genuine faiths, and that if they are, we can
learn from them even as they might learn from us.

As for the social character of the gospel, we seem to be
caught in a division between the denominational bureaucracy as the voice of this conviction and the congregations
whose programs are more oriented toward privatized religion than to public issues.

All of these cases of arrestment coalesce in the way our
present life is structured, a kind of clericalism in which the
clergy are the bearers of the modernist legacy and the laity
are on the outside. Promoting this structure is the way we
conceive of clergy education and church education. The
former educates in a rigorous and disciplined way, the latter nurtures, shapes, and forms but does not educate; and
since it does not, the heritage of critical modernism is
largely invisible and its themes puzzling and unclear to the
laity.

The final question concerns our calling in a situation of
decline. Given the anxiety a time of decline invokes, we
can anticipate one response to the heritage of modernism.
This, it says, is what has gotten us in trouble. To persist in
this heritage is what will do us in. It is true that the top
three so-called liberal denominations have declined the
most. But we must be cautious in our explanations of

this.[18] They are also the denominations with the lowest birthrates and with the largest numbers of young adults abandoning the church for something else. This is not a loss of members to conservative churches but a loss of the young to culture and secularity.[19] What is it about the mainline churches that accounts for this? It could be argued that it is their critical modernism, and a mood that prevents them from pressing religion on their young in authoritarian ways. But it is almost inconceivable that the young of these churches would be more attracted if the churches became narrowly denominational, unecumenical, indifferent to systemic social evils, pushing creation science and inerrant scriptures. What seems likely is that the critical modernism is more a mood, a set of deep convictions, which nevertheless are not communicated in the course of the education of the church. The result is that the mainline churches present to the young a set of confusions. Part of our calling, then, as a modernist church in hard times is the creation of a serious, rigorous program of education for the young in which the convictions of critical modernism and the interpretation of the gospel that attends them is clearly set forth.

But we must acknowledge the success, growth, and vitality of churches that do not hesitate to make absolute claims about themselves and their interpretations, who offer certainties, who make unabashed and even manipulative use of media technology. Religions tend to do well which develop specific pieties and casuistries and claim these are the very will of God and which make absolute claims for their traditions and institutions. The question is, are we in the business of religion? Our calling is not to religion but to faithfulness. It is not to growth and success but to a witness to the gospel. More specifically, our calling in a time of decline is to renew our deeper heritage as it has been carried into the themes of critical modernism. Perhaps not every Christian group has this calling. But some Christian communities must attest to the modern world an awareness that the Christian faith does not require rendering confessions, ancient authorities, and the denominational bearers of witness into absolutes, and some Christian communities must attest to the modern world that the Christian faith can exist in positive relation with the best knowledge of the time. Is this a strategic risk? Of course, since measured by quantity and success, all faithfulness is a risk. But here we must take our stand and say, even in these hard times, we can do no other.

3

Uncharted Territory: Congregational Identity and Mainline Protestantism

Barbara G. Wheeler

"What, if anything, can we do about this?" The question comes from Protestant church leaders who, aware for almost two decades that the mainline denominations have been declining in both membership and cultural influence, have recently been confronted with a burgeoning literature on the history and shape of their situation. The literature has generated more than usual interest. News publications have presented its conclusions in feature stories,[1] and many of the authors have been invited to speak at gatherings of church groups.[2] Church leaders' reactions to the messages contained in the recent studies have been sober. The denial and defensiveness one might expect in the face of such generally bad news have not been evident. After acknowledging the importance of the findings from recent research, and after admitting that the current problems are very serious, those who have responsibility for mainline Protestant institutions want something more than historical and social analysis. They want to know what, if anything, can be done.

The guidance church leaders seek is not so much about how to stem quantitative losses in membership, for most thoughtful Protestants know that numbers are not the central point. But institutional survival does matter, for without institutions to house them, the ideas and values that mainline traditions have held to be important will have no place in the broader cultural conversation. Further, membership decline has been accompanied by an apparent loss of religious vitality and sense of moral direction. Church leaders want to know not only what is likely to be the future of their institutions but also whether that deeper loss can be repaired. My purpose in this essay is to address those questions, with special emphasis on congregations. What can and should congregations do for themselves to assure their survival and integrity in the face of mainline decline, and what can and should denominational agencies do to assist them?

Religious Research and the Congregation

The assignment is a particularly interesting and challenging one, because its guiding question—How should mainline Protestant congregations respond to the difficult situations in which they find themselves?—leads one quickly into an area, that of congregational life in the mainline Protestantism, which has not been systematically investigated. Though the mainline Protestant congregation has been the target for much published advice and exhortation,[3] only a handful of studies have made it the focus of empirical investigation or interpretive analysis.[4] The pattern of neglect is curious, since despite the changes of the last two decades, mainline Protestant congregations remain a staple of religious life in this country and therefore, one would think, candidates for attention from researchers.

Recent developments in the study of American religion have, however, left the congregation stranded. Research on religious life seems to have forked into two main branches, each oriented in a direction that leaves the mainline congregation in a territory in between, in a kind of no-researchers'-land into which few paths for exploration have been cut.

One of these branches has been occupied with the study of local religious communities. Convinced that the essence of American religion is the local religious fellowship that gives the individual place and identity in the community,[5] a number of writers in recent years have produced intensive studies of local religious associations. Melvin Williams, for instance, has described in stunning detail the symbolic and social structures that create community in a Black Pentecostal church in Pittsburgh.[6] Nancy Ammerman has studied the social and conceptual mechanisms that give coherence to a fundamentalist Baptist congregation in the Northeast.[7] James Ault spent two years as a participant observer in a similar congregation of Baptist fundamentalists in New England and has captured the flavor of its religious and social life in the powerful film *Born Again.*[8] Other researchers have focused their attention on local manifestations of new and unconventional religions. Steven Tipton, for instance, in his book *Getting Saved from the Sixties,* describes how moral meaning was shaped for 1960s young people who joined a Zen Buddhist meditation center and a human potential group.[9]

The list of studies is by no means exhaustive. Perusal of recent journals and programs of researchers' meetings reveals other local religious associations that are popular subjects for investigation: Mormon stakes and wards, authoritarian cults like Jonestown, so-called New Age spiritual communities, and the Unification Church. But note that almost none of this burst of research energy has been expended in the description of mainline Protestant congregations.

There are a few exceptions. There are brief case studies, one of a Methodist church in the collection *Building Effective Ministry,* and several others used as illustrations in James Hopewell's book *Congregation.*[10] There is Steven Warner's recent book, *New Wine in Old Wineskins,* which is ostensibly a study of a Presbyterian church in northern California.[11] But this fascinating study is in fact focused primarily on an evangelical fellowship that starts outside the congregation and overruns it. The book introduces in vivid detail the young hippie evangelicals and their leader, but the Presbyterians who belonged to the church before the takeover and who quite surprisingly stayed on after it happened remain pale and shadowy. So *New Wine* too turns out to be a study of something other than a typical mainline congregation. In all my reading, I have found only one book, Michael Ducey's *Sunday Morning,* that looks at length and in depth at ordinary, long-established congregations that are allied with mainstream traditions.[12]

Why this neglect of mainline churches by scholars who are sharply aware of the importance of local expressions of religion? Evidently, these researchers are convinced that religious groups that keep their distance from modernity, whether by clinging to premodern forms of orthodoxy or by constructing antimodern theologies or postmodern spiritualities, have more to teach us about what it means to be a religious community than groups that have struggled to come to terms with modern ideas. Buried in that supposition may lurk a deeper one, that real religion is essentially supernaturalist, otherworldly, and in tension with modernity. Such a definition of religion renders most mainline churches something less than fully religious. If that view of religion is indeed in play, it is not surprising that mainline congregations are so rarely selected as fields for study by those who seek to understand how religion and community are mutually implicated.

The other major branch of research on American religion is focused not on local religious communities but on the broad religious movements that cut across local boundaries. Recently, this branch has been much occupied with reevaluating a favorite theory, one which holds that the direction of change in American religion is almost invariably toward the secular and away from the traditionally religious. That theory has lost some of its power to explain recent events. Why, these researchers are asking, if secularization is indeed the direction of religious change, has there been a resurgence of conservative religion at the end of the twentieth century? In addressing this vexing question, those who study broad movements have of course investigated the evangelical and conservative upsurge itself. But they have also paid plenty of attention to mainline religion. They have sought, in other words, to find out not only why conservative religion has proved so durable, but also why mainline traditions, which should be the religions of choice in an increasingly secular society, have fared so poorly.

The catalog of recent studies of mainline religion and its relation to other forms is a long one. It includes well-known works by Jeffrey Hadden, Dean Hoge, Jackson Carroll, Charles Glock, Rodney Stark, Martin Marty, Robert Bellah, William McKinney, Wade Clark Roof, and Robert Wuthnow.[13] The amount of research and writing on mainline Protestantism and the vigor of the discussion among the authors makes it all the more surprising that this branch of research has—like the other one—left the mainline local congregation almost untouched by investigative attention.

A clue to why the writers on mainline Protestantism have overlooked the congregation may be found in the methods used to produce many of the studies. Almost all of them probe religious movements by conducting or collating surveys of the attributes, attitudes, and practices of individuals.[14] Virtually all recent studies of what has happened to mainline Protestantism, including Wuthnow's magisterial book, rely on Gallup polls and other broad-scale surveys, all representing data collected from and describing the behavior of individuals. These surveys do ask individuals whether they belong to congregations, and some try to assess the quality and strength of the individual's ties to a congregation, but none of them looks directly at any actual congregations, to determine either what role congregations play in the movements under survey or how they are affected by those movements.

Underlying this pattern of almost always choosing the individual as the unit of analysis is another assumption about contemporary religion, different from the one that regulates community studies but just as strong. The assumption is that religious commitment in our time is chiefly an individual matter. In this view, the individual person, pushed and pulled by cultural tides and social forces, most of them originating outside institutions of organized religion, makes a decision about religious belief and adherence. Particular institutions like congregations are thus either the beneficiaries or the victims of individual choices, depending on how the decision-making process goes. Thus if we wish to understand contemporary religion, we must investigate the patterns of choice-making by studying the characteristics and attitudes of those who do the choosing. Religious communities and organizations enter this picture only at the end stage, as entities that are joined or deserted after the individual decision is made. Small wonder, then, that those who study mainline religion as a movement give congregations little attention in their research.

So the congregation has been neglected from two sides, and therefore the question of what congregations have to do with mainline decline is an exciting one. It invites researchers to do what they like most—to devise new research agendas and imagine adventuresome forays into unexplored regions. But, one must immediately add, because the necessary research has not even been begun, the question does not point in the direction of answers that might be available anytime soon.

Yet the church leaders' question, "What, if anything, can be done?" continues to press us. However exciting a topic may be that marks out a whole new area for research, and however much future studies may enrich our understanding of the congregation and American religion more generally, it will be tragic if the congregation languishes, like a patient with an interesting disease, while the studies are being conducted. Therefore, despite the fact that there is very little research that is directly relevant, it seems incumbent on those of us who study congregations to find something helpful to say to them and their leaders in the present situation, even if it must be tentative, hypothetical, and incomplete. Those of us who have adopted the mainline congregation as our focus for research must remember that congregations are not just interesting cases. They are also human communities that want to know what, if anything, they can do with the perplexing circumstances created by mainline difficulty and decline.

This essay, then, will attempt to look for clues, in the research on congregations and on American religion more broadly, that might give mainline churches guidance about what they can do. In the absence of a substantial body of research that bears directly on the matter, I propose to take a second look at some of the studies listed above. Many of them were intended for other purposes, but they may nonetheless yield suggestions, hints, and pointers about the role that the congregations of mainline Protestantism have played in recent developments and how they ought to respond. Perhaps these reports can tell us something, by inference or analogy if not directly, about the mostly uncharted territory of the mainline congregation.

What we shall be looking for in these reports are *theories* of the congregation, especially theories about the identity of congregations—what makes them what they are—for such theories may help us to understand what role congregations play in larger social and religious movements. Up until now, most strategies to stem decline at the local level have been based on anecdotes ("perhaps what worked in one place will work in another") or on a sort of fingers-crossed hopefulness ("maybe if we try *something* it will work"). A theory-based view of the congregation may provide a firmer basis for action.

Three Theories of the Congregation

One theory about what a congregation is and how it functions is set forth and illustrated in Stephen Warner's study of Mendocino Presbyterian Church. Warner went to Mendocino, California, in the early 1970s because he was concerned about his son by a former marriage, who along with Warner's former wife had become a charismatic and joined Mendocino Presbyterian. By the end of the decade, Warner had completed his study of the church and married the church's organist. His intimate connections yield an extraordinarily rich portrait. In the 1960s Mendocino had first a radical pastor, who opened the church to the local artistic community, and then a liberal pastor who took what turned out to be a fateful step: he urged Larry Redford, a high school teacher who had studied at Fuller Seminary and was seeking a focus for his intense evangelical commitments, to begin a ministry to the hippies who were flocking to the northern California coast. Redford's ministry, started as a commune, grew rapidly, was infused by refugees from other, even more intense evangelical groups in the area, and finally changed form into a charismatic fellowship of young couples, ex-hippies who had stopped using drugs and had bought property. Gradually the evangelicals joined the church and changed its character. In 1973, the congregation called an evangelical pastor, a man who, like their leader Redford, was a product of Fuller Seminary.

What paved the way for this revolution in an ordinary, rather sleepy Presbyterian church? Wrestling with that question led Warner to devise a complex interpretation about what was going on in Mendocino Presbyterian, and embedded in that interpretation is a theory about congregations and their role in religious movements.

The essence of the theory is that the congregation, except at rare moments, is a more or less inert structure, without internal dynamism. Joining many other theorists, Warner argues that societies alternate between states of exhilaration and routine. Powerful movements, such as waves of religious enthusiasm and tides of social change, create new institutions and revive old ones. Then these effervescent movements, which Warner calls "nascent states," die down, leaving behind institutions that reflect the structure of the nascent state, but that no longer take the movement's declared values "seriously and literally."[15] In fact, says Warner, the creative forces of the foregoing movement are "imprisoned"[16] in the institutions that remain.

In this view, established congregations are the precipitate of earlier movements of revival or reform. They are not exactly fossils, but the little power they have to move and act is leftover momentum from their nascent state. Essentially they are sluggish, conservative, almost-empty vessels, "old wineskins" in Warner's metaphor. They make few demands on their members, and they resist the infusion of new wine, whether from the right or the left. Mendocino had successfully resisted the efforts of its radical pastor, who left in discouragement. It gave way only under pressure from Redford, a natural leader with a sizable grass-roots movement behind him.[17] This too confirms Warner's theory, which gives a prominent role to the dynamic leaders who organize and inspire new social and religious movements.

The image of the congregation as a form or structure that has little vitality of its own and gets its identity from the outside emerges from other studies as well. Some writers, like Warner, view the congregation as the creation and container of external religious movements. Others emphasize the role played by nonreligious social forces in shaping the congregation and determining its identity. Beginning with the landmark research of H. Paul Douglass, a stream of studies has stressed the determining power of local context. "Social contextual factors" are so powerful, wrote Douglas Walrath in one such study, that "churches rarely escape their overwhelming influence."[18]

Robert Wuthnow, in his recent book, emphasizes how the character of congregational life has been shaped by broader trends. He describes how special-purpose religious groups have become more prominent and numerous in American life generally, and he suggests that local churches have adopted this pattern as "one of the important ways in which [they] evoke commitment from their members."[19] By providing lots of little groups, opportunities to join with others at the same stage in life or with similar commitments, the congregation puts out hooks to snag the interest of individuals who might otherwise find nothing to attract them into the congregational fellowship or to sustain their interest once they get there. Still other writers emphasize how the identity of congregations is shaped by external institutions such as seminaries, which train leaders who are inserted into congregational settings; and denominations, which provide programs, consultants, and sometimes money that buttress the congregation from the outside.

What all these views have in common is their portrayal of the congregation as a structure that has little dynamism of its own. The writers differ in their estimates of how the congregation will respond to external pressure. Some, like Warner, emphasize its resistance to outside forces, others point to its adaptability. But all join in the judgment that congregational character and identity are heavily determined from the outside. These contextual theories—for convenience we can group them as "wineskin theories"—hold that the congregation's identity is created, not by what it does, but by what is done to it.

Another, almost opposite view of the congregation emerges from the work of writers such as James Hopewell in his book *Congregation.* It was by accident that Hopewell, like Warner, came across congregations as a focus for research. A seminary professor who taught world religions, he became fascinated by the ways that a small Episcopal fellowship he had helped to start became a vigorous congregation despite his strong urging that it remain a small, informal worship group that would not compete with other churches in the area. What caused this growth into congregational form in the face of what Hopewell called his "unpromising" passive leadership? "Most of what constructed our congregation," he wrote, "did not occur by deliberate planning or goal setting; rather, a particular language developed among the members, an idiom that came to bind their actions and perspectives. Though its terms were drawn from the vast world repertoire of religious and social imagination, they were particularized in a local language that expressed our own views, values, and actions. Together we wove a network of audible and physical signs that, informed by humanity's symbolic struggles for community, now shaped our own."[20]

As he studied several other churches, Hopewell became convinced that every congregation develops a powerful and particular idiom that both holds it together and "distinguishes it from others around it and like it. Even a plain church on a pale day," he insisted, "catches one in a deep current of narrative interpretation and representation by which people give sense and order to their lives."[21] Narrative, in fact, is the key in Hopewell's view. Congregations are richly idiomatic subcultures that construct narratives, dramatic frameworks that give them coherence and identity. These narrative frameworks hold in place several elements, including a worldview, which is an account of reality that serves as the backdrop for the local story; a character, which is the set of dispositions and values that make up the congregation's ethos; and of course a plot, the march of events that mark the congregation's passage through time. In Hopewell's account, congregations scavenge the whole of their life together for bits and pieces of custom to weave into a local culture and story that is theirs alone. Explicitly religious symbols and ideas play a part, but so do homely, everyday events and customs—the kind of doughnuts served at the coffee hour, the death of the pastor's baby son, the fight about whether to accept a large gift from a longtime patron for a new building no one else wants. The emotions, behavior patterns, tastes, sights, and smells that these events and customs entail all are knit into a tight fabric that Hopewell calls the congregation's larger liturgy.

This ritualized story has magnetic power. It draws in people who want to be associated with the mood, values, and worldview built into it. We join one congregation rather than another of the same denomination or socioeconomic status, and we stay in that congregation, Hopewell suggests, because we want to participate in the unique dramatic enactment that congregation offers.

Hopewell illustrates this theory with several accounts of congregations that emphasize their narrative structure and symbolic and mythic resonances. He tells, for instance, of a young but somnolent Methodist congregation in a growing but still heavily wooded suburb, a church that, like the mythic character Sleeping Beauty or Briar Rose, has devised prickly defenses against any ministerial suitors that might try to wake it up. Much more than by location or denomination or ossified tradition, Hopewell maintains, that Methodist church's identity has been created by the web of symbols, stories, and meanings that its participants have constructed.[22]

This is, of course, a very different representation of the congregation. The congregation's identity, that which makes it what it is, is formed, not by forces that either buffet or shore up the church from the outside, but by a process within, the construction of local culture and narrative, that occurs inevitably in any group that persists over time. And indeed, Hopewell argues, the meaningfulness of the congregation is inevitable. When people congregate, they construct a culture. Without the glue of a meaning-making culture, congregations, especially now that church membership is not a social expectation, would simply fly apart. But significant numbers of them do not, even though a confluence of forces threatens their survival. Warner thinks that the weight of a dead tradition keeps them in existence. Hopewell, in contrast, insists that their capacity for creating narratively structured cultures is what makes them durable.

Some other recent writers on congregations proceed from assumptions similar to Hopewell's about what constitutes a congregation. In Nancy Ammerman's interpretation of the fundamentalists she studied, for instance, the congregation offers a language and meaning system for wanderers who otherwise would struggle, and perhaps fail, to sustain as individuals their refusal "to grant the modern world legitimacy."[23] Similarly, Melvin Williams' Black Pentecostals find in Zion Church both a structure of human relationships and a cornucopia of metaphors that enable them, refugees from the rural South, to survive in inner-city Pittsburgh. In both these views, the congregation gets most of the shape and content of its local culture from elsewhere and then configures those materials in a distinctive way. Thus Williams and Ammerman make fewer claims than Hopewell does about the uniqueness of particular congregations. But all three share the conviction that the congregation is a crucible of meaning, a vital community that has sufficient coherence and intensity to affect the lives of its members and sometimes even its wider environment.

Because the congregation as a cultural institution has dynamism of its own, this perspective places less emphasis on leadership than a view like Warner's. Ethos—the mood, atmosphere, tone, and values of a social group—develops slowly, and though ethos and culture do change, sudden cultural revolutions are rare. Deep structures, language patterns, and core values tend to persist, even through periods of great turbulence. Thus new leaders with their distinctive ways of doing things are far more likely to be incorporated into the local culture, in this perspective, than they are to transform it.

A third theory of the congregation stands between the two views just described of how congregational identity is formed. A good example of the third approach is found in Michael Ducey's book *Sunday Morning,* a study of how four churches in the Lincoln Park neighborhood of Chicago responded to the upheaval in that formerly German community created by racial and ethnic change, youth gangs like the Young Lords, and the demonstrations surrounding the 1968 Democratic Convention. Ducey's special focus is worship. He analyzes patterns of religious ritual in the four congregations in an effort to understand why one of them, the United Methodist Church of the Three Crosses, completely reconstructed its worship services in an attempt to give religious meaning to current events, while another, St. Paul's (United Church of Christ), tried to respond but then returned to its earlier patterns, and two others, one Roman Catholic and the other Missouri Synod Lutheran, simply shut out the chaos and attempted no changes at all.

Ducey's four churches were similar in significant ways. All were German at their founding and had become

English-speaking and middle-class. They were located within a few blocks of each other. Why, then, did they respond to similar pressures so differently? Ducey offers a theory of the congregation in response to that question. One element of the theory sounds like the old and empty wineskins view. Ducey suggests that in complex societies like ours, traditional religious symbols and formulas tend to lose their meaning, since that meaning is usually established in childhood, and people's early religious experiences are now so various that by the time they gather as adults in congregations, "common feelings based on that period of life cannot support any but the most general symbols, such as the cross [or] . . . calling oneself Christian." But to symbolize group solidarity, says Ducey, takes something more, "a full set of religious-cultural artifacts."[24] In crises like the ones confronting Lincoln Park churches in the late 1960s, the incapacity of general and one-dimensional symbols to provide coherence in the face of chaos becomes very evident. In such situations a special form of authority, which Ducey calls "charisma," is required to keep the congregation from coming apart. This sounds a lot like Warner. Congregations are empty shells that lack meaning-making capacity, so authority figures are required to import meaning and moral direction into them.

But Ducey's understanding of charisma is complex, so he sees a range of possibilities for dealing with the congregation's problem of anomie, its immobilization in meaninglessness. Some churches, like the Catholic and Lutheran ones in his study, will continue to rely on their designated leaders to tell them what the church or denomination's official doctrinal teachings say their symbols mean. Warner would not think this much of a solution, since in his view denominations and the traditions they represent are also old wineskins.[25] Ducey largely agrees. He thinks unlikely, though not impossible, that the symbolic life of these congregations will be enriched by leaders playing the traditional role of interpreters of tradition. But this pattern is not the only possibility. Alternatively, a congregation might rely on its ordained leader to mediate between the interpretation of symbols in the orthodox tradition and the more personal interpretations offered by members. This is what happened at St. Paul's UCC: its minister tried to enrich its rituals by reconstructing them in part, using "fragmentary information" he had gathered about how his members were finding order and meaning in the turbulence around them.[26] But the fragments were too diverse, and the new pieces of ritual scattered among the old forms served not to express solidarity but to symbolize the lack of it. Rather than face that unsettling reality, the congregation decided to return to its old, highly traditional worship patterns, which at least *appeared* unified. A third response to symbolic emptiness was enacted at the Church of the Three Crosses. Encouraged by the minister, the members decided to use their own charismatic authority to imbue their worship with symbolic significance and to link it to the social upheaval in their neighborhood. They changed the arrangement of space, the language, music, texts, style of spoken delivery, choreography and costume, all in the direction of making the worship more participatory, egalitarian, and rich in local meaning. In other words, they made themselves a culture and rituals to express it. This sounds like Hopewell and the others who view congregations as cultures or subcultures. But there is a significant difference. In Ducey's theory, dynamism and vitality do not occur naturally in the act of gathering and sticking together over time. Congregations, if they seek depth and richness in their common life, have to choose to create them.

For want of a better term, one might call Ducey's a voluntary theory of congregational identity. Other writers have proposed similar views. Some, for instance, have written about congregations as "open systems" whose identity is determined by the interplay of external forces and an internal capacity to resist pressure from outside and sometimes to act upon their environment.[27] The most famous of the voluntary theories is Dean Kelley's, which holds that churches may be weak or strong. Weak churches are permissive and pluralistic. Strong churches are those that make a decision to get into gear, to struggle out of their weakness by demanding a high degree of loyalty and commitment from their members and offering a seamless belief system in return.[28] None of these theories is entirely clear about why some congregations activate this internal potential and others do not. But the role of leadership does seem to be important. Leaders in this view do not themselves bring new life into the congregation, as in the wineskin view; nor do they simply pass through cultures that were formed long before and will persist long after their tenure. Rather, leaders play a catalytic role: they goad into action others who, if the leader did not intervene, would remain passive and marginally involved.

What, If Anything, Can We Do?

These three theories about how congregational identity is formed yield different readings of the role congregations have played in creating the current situation of mainline churches.

In the body of theory that portrays the congregation as an empty vessel, congregations have played no significant role at all. Decline has happened to them. Since by definition they are the structural vestige of earlier religious movements, somewhat reshaped by current social forces, they have simply sat on the sidelines and watched as a series of unfavorable social and demographic developments and a religious revival at war with their tradition have eroded their base of support in the culture.

In the voluntary view, mainline congregations and the denominations with which they are aligned have contributed actively to their own decline. By their complacency and laziness, or, according to Kelley, their promiscuous chasing after current fads like ecumenism and social relevance, they have permitted the energy and coherence they once contained to leak out.

The cultural view is murkier on this point, because those who hold it give very little attention to the relationship of the congregational subculture to anything outside the congregation. But if pressed, the culture theorists would probably argue that the current studies of decline put the emphasis in the wrong place. What is significant, they would say, is not how the mainline has been reduced, which is easily explained by current social and cultural trends, but how the tradition has persisted in a variety of local forms amid conditions that are so hostile to it.

So what, given these different readings of decline, can be done? What courses of action are open to congregations, their leaders, and the outside agencies that support them? The theories are very general, and the research undergirding them is very partial and scattered, so none of them provides a precise game plan. But each one does imply different expectations for the future and suggests a different set of possible responses.

The wineskin view leaves us subdued if not depressed about the future. It forces us to face the fact that the time is not ripe for mainline renewal. Most social and demographic trends seem, in fact, to be moving in the opposite direction.[29] Nor are there signs on the horizon of some new state of religious enthusiasm that might revivify mainline institutions in short order.

Since social movements will not naturally bolster mainline congregations and since the kind of religious revival that would benefit them is unlikely, the wineskin view leaves those who lead congregations with only one choice: to adapt. That is, of course, something mainline congregations have been doing. They have adapted to their changing circumstances both intuitively, as Wuthnow has suggested, and as a conscious strategy. But the studies we have been reviewing suggest that some of the approaches to adaptation have been misguided. Those who stress the power of local context would be critical of the mainline denominations' tendency to typecast churches by their contexts—urban, suburban, rural—and to depend on standardized guides to change for each contextual type, without paying sufficient attention to the very different local setting of each congregation. The research also suggests that it is a mistake to spend too much energy catching up with what has already happened. "Congregations that thrive amid change," says Douglas Walrath, "generally are those that are able to relate effectively . . . to the context's future rather than hanging on to a past that . . . is bound to vanish."[30] Successful adaptation, he argues, results from joining a movement in formation, rather than refitting to accommodate one that has already occurred. So do your own homework, say these theorists; study closely the changes in your particular environment to which you might adapt. And try to figure out not only what has already occurred but also what is likely to happen next.

Finally, the wineskin theorists instruct, remember that adaptation takes a certain kind of leader, someone who can help to orient a congregation open to possible sources of new vitality and direction outside itself. Even Warner, who thinks that real change is likely to be of the revolutionary sort, acknowledges the importance of a kind of John the Baptist figure like Mendocino's liberal pastor, who opened the church to all kinds of new participants and thus paved the way for more profound changes to come. Often we have counseled pastors to adopt an aggressively prophetic style to get congregations to look outside themselves. These theorists suggest that this is a mistake. Steadiness and moderation are preferable. Most adaptive change, especially if it involves difficult transitions across boundaries of race, economic class, or age, is exceedingly slow. Leaders who are patient and can set modest expectations are critical for adaptive success.

The voluntary approach sets a different mood and agenda for action. It provides mainline congregations with reason for optimism about their future. Local churches in this view have the capacity not only to conform to developments in their environment, but even more, to transform themselves into vivid expressions of the traditions they carry from the past. Such transformation is not, as we have seen, guaranteed. In fact, congregations are more likely than not to sink into passivity and frustration as they watch their leaders try, and usually fail, to bring to life ancient ideas and symbols that have been drained of contemporary meaning. A few congregations experiment timidly with new rituals and patterns of action but finally return to older and safer ways. Stories of successful transformation are rare. Thus when we take the voluntary view we are more likely to feel guilty about the past than cheerful about the future.

But still this view holds out hope and some suggestions about strategy for those committed to renewal. The hope is congregational transformation, and like adaptation, it is not a new idea. For at least the last twenty years, a small army of consultants has been offering techniques that promise to bring it about. Usually these techniques have not worked or have had only temporary effects. Again, the studies we have looked at suggest that one problem in our past efforts has been our reliance on standardization. Many mainline congregations seem to be weak and lifeless, and it is tempting to look for one prescription that will work for all of them, but the problem takes a different shape in every setting. Thus there is no effective battery of four or five or twelve easy developmental steps to revitalization that will work everywhere. So put aside the handbooks, say the voluntary theorists, and focus on the art of leadership for transformation.

Here too, the theorists suggest, we have been retailing the wrong ideas about leadership. We have portrayed ministry in a dualistic way: on the one hand, as the modern science of conflict management and group therapy to heal congregational wounds, and on the other, as the traditional source of special teaching authority. But if we really want to galvanize congregations to recreate themselves as centers of meaning and moral direction, we need something else: not conflict managers, but leaders who are willing to endure conflict, for only in crises does the need for the reconstruction of meaning become acute; not authority figures, but leaders who are prepared to forego any special personal authority and charisma that comes with the ministerial role and to function instead as protective figures who have the wit and skill to recognize leadership in others and to arrange for that leadership to be exercised. Only a leader willing to take the risks of enduring crisis and sharing authority, according to voluntary theory, can stimulate a congregation to reconstruct its symbols, beliefs, and ways of being in the world.

In the cultural view, which is a perspective that mainline Protestants have not typically taken, the future looks viable though not bright. The cultural view does not promise revival or new growth, but it does emphasize the congregation's capacity for *being there,* for continuing to exist despite massive changes around it.

The cultural view suggests not so much a strategy as a posture or attitude that should govern strategy. It portrays congregations as communities that are the primary sites of religious traditions, not because someone imported those traditions, as in the wineskin view, but because these are the centers in which traditions are actually formed. More than seminaries or denominational structures, which play a part in constructing traditions but which have privileges that insulate them from some of the consequences of doing that, congregations are the places where, in the ugly but apt phrase, the rubber meets the road, where the struggle to find religious meaning in a chaotic world occurs in the most complete and complicated way. Any congregation that has woven a more universally practiced tradition into the fabric of its local culture has, in this perspective, arrived at a solution, however homely and idiosyncratic, to the problem of religious belief and commitment in modern circumstances. As a result, congregations know something that the rest of us—researchers, church officials, and even many ministers—do not know about what it takes for mainline religion to survive in times like these. If this is the case, we ought to be approaching congregations quite differently than we currently do. We ought to be trying to learn from them. How do they accomplish the construction of meaning, filled as they are with ordinary people under extraordinary pressures. What enables them to persist in adverse conditions?

The cultural theorists would advise those who are leaders of congregations to become cultural investigators. Like an anthropologist entering a village, these leaders must observe and listen while participating in the congregation's activities. The goal is to discover the strategy for survival and renewal that is already embedded in the congregation's culture. Usually the congregation will not be able to articulate this strategy. Even if it can, it probably will not value it very highly, since congregations too often accept the wider view that they are empty of meaning and selfishly preoccupied.

The task of the leader, in the cultural view, is to harvest the local knowledge that the congregation cannot express or judges to be unimportant, to bring it to consciousness and give it shape. In preaching, teaching, and organizing, the congregation must be shown what Hopewell would call its genius, its unique way of holding itself together as it has struggled to find meaning and moral direction. Then, working with what is already there, the leader must help the congregation envision how its triumphs and failures point to a distinctive future.

Our three theories about congregations have yielded three lines of strategy. Search the context and adapt to it, say the wineskin theorists. Goad the whole community into action, into remaking old symbols in contemporary form, say those who take the voluntary view. Mine the riches that are already present in the congregation's local culture, say those who view the congregation as culture. But a problem remains. How do leaders—pastors, seminary students and those who teach them, lay church leaders and denominational officers—decide what to do in actual situations? Which of these quite different approaches should you take?

To some extent, your choices will be guided by your theological convictions. Adaptation makes good sociological sense, and it presents theological opportunities to encounter the ways Christ is working in culture, but your theological principles may lead you to set limits: You may be convinced that there are some social and cultural trends to which Christian congregations must not adapt. The kind of

transformation that involves the whole congregation in reforming traditions accords with both sophisticated organizational theory and with much in contemporary theologies
of ministry; but if carried to extremes, the process may
seem to some to spread authority too widely, opening the
way for extreme or faddish ideas. Searching for and inter-
preting the local cultural knowledge of congregations takes
seriously the international character of Christian belief as
well as recent insights about the power of culture, but some
will be disturbed by the absence in that approach of a critical standpoint from which to judge culture.

Your theological convictions will help you make choices,
but they do not solve the empirical and practical part of
your problem. Which of these strategies is best grounded?
Which is most likely to work? Those questions return us to
the situation described at the beginning of this essay. Because the mainline congregation has not been directly
studied, because we are in uncharted territory, *we do not
know with any certainty how mainline congregations
should respond to their current perplexing situation.* Until
we do, those who are immediately accountable to congregations, namely, pastors and lay leaders, will have to proceed as researchers in the field. You will have to decide
which of these theories, or what synthesis of several of
them, best interprets a particular situation.

Having left you with only hypotheses, pointers, and your
own seasoned judgment to respond to the good but difficult
case of the congregation, those of us who serve in seminaries and denominational agencies have some responsibilities
we *must* begin to take seriously. We deserve a good part of
the blame for the fact that the congregation has been left
high and dry in the world of research. Denominations and
interdenominational agencies, once the centers for studies
of congregations, have reduced their research departments
to skeletons and assigned them to do statistical record-
keeping and market research for denominational programs.
Seminaries and academic guilds, which once supplied researchers to participate in church-sponsored studies, have
replaced the congregation on faculty research agendas, tak-

ing up more abstract concerns now that sponsorship for congregational studies is no longer available from denominations. If we, scholars and decision makers whose primary concern is the well-being of the mainline churches, find it so easy to overlook our pivotal institution, the congregation, it should hardly be surprising that secular researchers minimize its importance.

It is time to correct this situation. Seminaries and denominations must lead the way in focusing careful and comprehensive research attention on the congregation. We owe it to those who spend their lives in congregational leadership to provide more theory and practical guidance for their work. Even more fundamentally, we owe it to the tradition that we are committed to serve, and to the values and deep beliefs embedded in it. Theological ideas and organizational structures, important as they are, cannot sustain a reformed and reforming tradition. It is carried now, as it has been in the past, by communities gathered in fellowship with Christ. We must seek to understand—at much greater depth and with much more sensitivity than before—the communities that have called and nurtured us all in the love, knowledge, and service of God.

4

On Dropping the Subject: Presbyterians and Sabbath Observance in the Twentieth Century

Benton Johnson

Most modern Presbyterians would consider the subject of this essay, namely the question of how the Lord's Day should be observed, trivial.

It has been many years since most Presbyterians have paid serious attention to this question. Nothing concerning it appears in the official pronouncements of any of the six General Assemblies held since the reunion of 1983, and neither of the uniting denominations had said anything about it since 1963. What is more, scholars have shown little interest in the drift of Protestant opinion and practice concerning the Lord's Day during our own times. There are major scholarly works on how Scottish Presbyterians and English Puritans viewed the Sabbath,[1] and there is a respectable literature on the rise and progress of Sabbatarianism in America, but virtual silence reigns on the fate of the Sabbath since roughly the time of the First World War. Ernest Trice Thompson touched on the matter in his monumental work on Presbyterians in the South,[2] James H. Smylie reflected briefly on it in 1980,[3] and Louis Weeks wrote a valuable essay on the biblical foundations of Sabbath pronouncements made by southern Presbyterians,[4] but one searches in vain for a really comprehensive treatment. Scholars, too, seem to regard the story of the Sabbath in our own times as a trivial matter.

Why, then, should I choose a subject of such small significance? In my opinion, a look at the record of how Presbyterians have regarded the Sabbath in recent generations will give us an opportunity to reflect in new ways on the vexing problem of church decline and the prospects for its reversal, for in the story of what has happened to the Sabbath we can discern a paradigm for a broad process of change not only within Presbyterianism but within the Protestant community at large. I cannot tell that story in full, for neither I nor anyone else has done the painstaking work needed to bring it to light. But I have examined in some detail the minutes of General Assemblies for most of the twentieth century,[5] and I believe they contain some major themes of its "plot." These General Assembly minutes not only provide a year-by-year record of official pronouncements, they also provide strong hints of what Presbyterians back home have been thinking and doing.

Presbyterians and the Sabbath: The Old View

Most Presbyterians with deep roots in their tradition have a sense that their forebears took the observance of Sunday much more seriously than it is taken today. Their image of that older Sabbath is one of strict rules and regulations aimed at the suppression of all enjoyment and spontaneity. In the past, in fact, many members of the general public associated this grim view of the Lord's Day specifically with Presbyterianism, which became the butt of many popular jokes. The celebrated agnostic Robert Ingersoll was raised a Presbyterian and he held that denomination in special disesteem to the end of his days. "No church," he once wrote, "has done more to fill the world with gloom than the Presbyterian." "Nothing ever was, nothing ever will be," he declared, "more disgusting than a Puritan Sunday."[6] The perception that Presbyterianism is a stern and sour faith was shared by many of Ingersoll's Christian contemporaries. It was a theme of several novels of the late nineteenth century, including Margaret Deland's 1888 best-seller *John Ward, Preacher.*[7] It is no wonder that modern Presbyterians, if they have learned of their heritage from sources such as these, are grateful that times have changed.

But if one examines Presbyterian sources themselves, a somewhat different picture of the old Sabbath emerges. To be sure, Presbyterians never thought of the Sabbath as a day for golf or swimming, or even as a day for mystical experience of the divine. They approached the holy day, as serious Presbyterians still approach many things, with a commitment to obey the will of God, to conform to the mind of Christ. Presbyterians and others in the Reformed tradition held that Christ's teaching and his sacrifice did not abolish the basic principles of the Mosaic law, including the Fourth Commandment. The law is no longer a means of justification before God, but it remains as a rule of life. In fact, those who are justified are empowered for a life of service to God and humanity with the law and Christ's example as their basic guide. Though each sphere of life has a measure of autonomy, no sphere is off-limits to the dominion of God's will. The state must not teach theology and the church cannot enact laws for civil society, but God's will must guide them both, just as it must inform art, literature, personal morality—and the use of time. So far as I know, the Presbyterian Church has never repudiated the basic contours of this position.

In the older Presbyterian interpretation, however, the Sabbath was, in the words of McGuffey's *Sixth Reader,* "the keystone of the arch which sustains the temple of virtue." "The Sabbath," the reader declares, "lies at the foundation of all true morality. . . . We may not, at once, perceive the effects which this weekly observance produces. Like most moral causes, it operates slowly; but it operates surely, and gradually weakens the power and breaks the yoke of profligacy and sin." This was Blackstone's view, it was Lord Chief Justice Hale's view, and it was the view of numerous public figures in American life, including at least one justice of the U.S. Supreme Court.[8]

Translated into the language of modern sociology, this means that a commitment to the moral code of Presbyterianism, or indeed of any other religion, does not sustain itself automatically but requires a periodic and public reinforcement by means of a regimen of symbolic work that is separate and distinct from ordinary work. The Sabbath was both personal and social in its intentions: it was personal in its attempt to secure the continued allegiance of individuals to the faith, and it was social in its emphasis on the moral rules that bound family, church, and political community alike. The Sabbath symbolized God's dominion over all spheres of the common life.

This was the dominant view among Presbyterians one hundred years ago, and it persisted in some Presbyterian circles well into the twentieth century. For example, when Sunday newspapers with their comic supplements became popular in the 1890s, both the northern and the southern General Assemblies emphatically condemned them as an alien invasion of sacred time.[9] A report to the southern General Assembly of 1914 declared the Sabbath to be of "vital importance to the life and prosperity of the Church, to the welfare of our country and the propagation of our religion" (GA, PCUS, 1914, p. 75). Twenty years later, another report declared that "it is to be doubted if the WORD could survive the complete destruction of the Sabbath" (GA, PCUS, 1934, p. 90). Time and again General Assemblies approved reports and adopted recommendations containing such phrases as these: "This nation cannot survive unless the Christian Sabbath is observed" (GA, PCUS, 1933, p. 34); "The Christian home, the Bible, and the Sabbath are the three units of the Christian Gibralter [sic]" (GA, PCUS, 1936, p. 71); "The observance of the Lord's Day . . . is vital to the safety and security of the Church, the home and the nation" (GA, PCUS, 1937, p. 115); "God's Name, God's Book, God's Son, God's Church, and God's Day are ESSENTIAL factors in the spiritual life of the individual, the Church, and the nation" (GA, PCUS, 1944, p. 162); and finally, one of my favorites: *"Let us beware, brethren:* As goes the Sabbath, so goes the church, as goes the church, so goes the nation" (GA, PCUS, 1948, p. 183).

In view of this linkage between faith, the church, morality, and the national community, it is not surprising that some Presbyterians urged both the civil authorities and private business to help safeguard the Sabbath. In 1816, for example, the General Assembly protested the transportation of the U.S. mail on the Lord's Day and asked Presbyterians in all Congressional districts to work for repeal of the law that permitted it. This was only the first in a long line of General Assembly pronouncements to public and private agencies on the subject of the Sabbath (GA, PCUSA, 1932, pp. 168–169). Presbyterian Assemblies beseeched the operators of the Philadelphia Centennial Exposition of 1876, the Chicago World's Fair of 1893, and the Panama-Pacific Exposition of 1915, to close their gates on Sunday.[10] In 1918 the northern Assembly saluted Governor Charles S. Whitman, of New York, a Presbyterian deacon and the son of a Presbyterian minister. The church "is proud," the Assembly announced, "of its sons in public life who stand so decidedly for great fundamental American and Christian principles." The governor had recently given assurance that he would veto any bill the legislature passed that would weaken the state's Sabbath laws (GA, PCUSA, 1918, p. 103).

One finds fewer pronouncements of this sort in the minutes of southern General Assemblies, owing to the fact that for generations that denomination held the view that ecclesiastical courts must not "intermeddle" in civil affairs. But when its General Assembly did "intermeddle," it was often on behalf of the public observance of the Lord's Day. The southern church endorsed national prohibition only once,[11] but on numerous occasions it addressed federal officials or made recommendations for federal legislation on matters related to the Sabbath.[12] Moreover, in 1878 the southern church was the first of the two major Presbyterian bodies to establish a permanent committee on Sabbath observance, and it pioneered in efforts to organize a consortium of Protestant denominations to promote Sabbath observance in the nation at large (GA, PCUS, 1931, p. 157). These efforts proved premature, but in December 1888 it joined with the northern Presbyterians and other mainline bodies in organizing the American Sabbath Union, whose commission it was to make Sunday a national day of rest through exhortation and political action. For several generations it commanded the active support of all the major Presbyterian denominations. In 1908, perhaps to broaden its appeal, the American Sabbath Union changed its name to the Lord's Day Alliance.[13]

Although its history is yet to be written,[14] the Lord's Day Alliance, in cooperation with labor organizations and even with Catholic groups, helped secure many new Sunday laws,[15] especially during the first two decades of the twentieth century. It is sometimes supposed that in the Gilded Age Sabbath laws were both strict and strictly enforced, but the truth is a bit different. In 1914 the northern General Assembly recalled that when its permanent Sabbath committee was established in 1891, "comparatively few of the States had Sabbath laws; to-day 47 of the 48 States [have passed such laws]." Never, it went on to say, had legislatures and law enforcement officers been so receptive to Sabbath observance, or "captains of industry and employers of labor so willing to listen to the needs of labor" (GA, PCUSA, 1914, p. 219). There followed almost five pages of recent triumphs under the heading, "Victories During the Year" (GA, PCUSA, 1914, pp. 219–224). At the height of the Progressive Era, Presbyterians were in the forefront of a new national effort to safeguard Sunday for the church and for the family both by persuasion and by civil legislation.

Sounding the Alarm

But times were already changing. In 1918, in a report that was seventeen pages long, the northern General Assembly viewed with alarm the mounting pressure to exempt commercial baseball games and movies from the

Sunday closing laws. A former President of the United States had come out for the exemption, and so had the governor of a midwest state (GA, PCUSA, 1918, p. 92). "The enemy is everywhere organized and his mighty drives have begun with greater intensity than ever before," the report warned (p. 91). "The battleground of the churches during the next 10 years," it declared, "will be on the field of the Christian Sabbath" (p. 91). It urged everyone to give generously to the cause, for *"all the other benevolent enterprises of the Church hang for support on the security of the Lord's Day. See I Cor. 16:22"* (p. 93; emphasis in the original). Three years later the same Assembly condemned "the organized attack on the Lord's Day in putting on the so-called 'Blue Law' propaganda last November, the purpose of which was to discredit the Lord's Day Alliance, the intermediary of the churches in the development of Sabbath Observance" (GA, PCUSA, 1921, p. 61).

In the 1920s and 1930s the northern General Assembly continued to make new proposals for a better public observance of the Lord's Day,[16] but it reported fewer victories and the tone of its pronouncements became more and more pessimistic. Sabbath desecration was evidently on the increase. In 1931 the northern General Assembly urged efforts to "prevent the encroachment of a conscienceless commercialism on the American Sunday" (GA, PCUSA, 1931, p. 60). Two years later it complained of "the lure of Sunday diversions and amusements" and worried—correctly, as it turned out—about "a possible invasion of the Christian Sabbath by the dangerous drink evil" (PCUSA, 1933, p. 163). The next year it complained about "news stands open on Sunday with obscene and salacious books on sale" (GA, PCUSA, 1934, p. 197). After the southern church reestablished its Permanent Committee on the Sabbath in 1931,[17] that committee produced a long series of reports on the trend toward the defilement of Sunday and warnings of what would happen if it were not reversed. In 1934 the committee wrote that "the misuse and desecration of the Sabbath . . . besmears it with the utterly callous mire and filth of hopeless selfishness" and "nails a question mark upon the Cross itself" (GA, PCUS, 1934, pp. 90, 92).

In the 1940s the reports grew more strident and frantic in tone. In 1942, the committee bemoaned the fact that "Sunday . . . has become a wide open day. . . . Motion picture theatres, sports of every sort, automobile joy riding, night clubs, pool rooms and places where spiritous liquors can be bought . . . " (GA, PCUS, 1942, p. 139). That same year, in response to an overture from the Presbytery of Cherokee, the General Assembly sent President Roosevelt a page of Bible verses supporting Sabbath observance—all of them written in capital letters (GA, PCUS, 1942, pp. 36, 83, 93–94). Capital letters showed up again the next year, this time in the report of the Standing Committee, which pointed to the "DISTRESSING NEGLECT AND TREMENDOUS PROFANATION OF THIS SACRED DAY . . . " (GA, PCUS, 1943, p. 89). Three more lines of capital letters appear in the Permanent Committee's report the next year (GA, PCUS, 1946, pp. 41, 96). In 1947 the Permanent Committee expressed grave concern that with the war now ended, the "Continental Sunday" would become the norm in America (GA, PCUS, 1947, p. 96). And in 1948 its report described the modern use of Sunday as one of "NEGLECT AND DESECRATION; THE DOING OF WHATEVER KIND OF WORK SEEMS WORLDLY PROFITABLE; A HOLIDAY FOR WORLDLY PLEASURE"—once again, all in capital letters (GA, PCUS, 1948, p. 183).

A Change at the Grass Roots

To old-line Sabbatarians, allowing movie houses and beer halls to operate on Sunday was bad enough, but it was far worse for Presbyterians themselves to patronize them on the Lord's Day. In the past, General Assemblies had sometimes expressed the wish that Presbyterians would attend church more regularly or that they would observe the Sabbath more faithfully, but after World War I such wishes and concerns began showing up more frequently in General Assembly minutes. The northern church minutes for 1918 contain the following:

> A pastor in New York State said to me: "When Saturday night came I used to pray for a clear Sabbath so that I might see my people fill up the Church. Now, when Saturday night comes, I don't know how to pray. If I pray for a clear day many of my people will go automobiling. If I pray for a rainy day they will give the rainy day as an excuse to stay home" (GA, PCUSA, 1918, p. 95).

But this is only a mild and humorous warning of what was to come. By the mid-1930s both General Assemblies were expressing alarm at the growing violation of the Sabbath by Presbyterians themselves. In 1933 the northern Assembly noted "the alarming departure from formerly fixed habits of public worship, the loss of the family altar and the lure of Sunday diversions and amusements" (GA, PCUSA, 1933, p. 163). The next year the southern church began stepping up its efforts to promote Sabbath observance among its own people (GA, PCUS, 1934, p. 92; 1935, pp. 96–97), but evidently without much success, for by 1942 the Permanent Committee on the Sabbath was once again expressing alarm that Presbyterians were not keeping the Lord's Day in a proper manner. In 1948 the Committee announced that the greatest threat to the Sabbath was "the apathy on the part of a large element of our church members who make no effort to combat the evil forces. . . . These piously recite the Ten Commandments, the confession and creeds, observe the sacrifices and feasts on a Sabbath morning; [then] go to movies, the races or athletic contests on the afternoon; to a cocktail party in the evening; and to the polls the following election day to vote for the so-called 'open Sunday'; what a sorry spectacle" (GA, PCUS, 1948, p. 183). "Is there uncertainty as to the meaning of the [Fourth] Commandment?" another Committee asked. "Is the language ambiguous? Certainly not." "To all who have grown liberal . . . we would lovingly say, Brethren, let us repent" (GA, PCUS, 1943, p. 150).

The Committees were undoubtedly responding to a real

trend among Presbyterians at large. A profound shift toward secularism and freedom from traditional moral restraints took place in the nation at large in the aftermath of World War I. The public ridicule of religion that accompanied the shift was directed almost exclusively at the very tradition of which Presbyterianism was a leading exemplar. Prohibition, blue laws, and "Puritan" standards of conduct were belittled in the press, in popular literature, on the stage, and in the movies. An insight into the cultural shift as it affected Presbyterians was, I suspect, contained in a remarkable report which the Sabbath committee of the southern church prepared for the 1939 General Assembly. The committee observed that "We live in a time when everything is being reconsidered. Nothing is accepted because it is old. The general idea is that whatever is is probably wrong." Moreover, within the church it is the youth who are most likely to question traditional ways. "To the aging whose raising has been strict," the old standards for Sabbath observance seem proper and well founded, but "the young, whose surroundings are different," have serious questions about traditional Presbyterian positions on many things. In other words, there was intellectual and spiritual ferment in the church, and it was centered among the youth.[18]

Dropping the Subject

The processes were already at work that would lead Presbyterians to drop the whole subject of the Sabbath. All through the 1920s and 1930s the northern General Assembly issued annual statements on the Sabbath. But compared to the statements adopted in the first two decades of this century, these postwar pronouncements were remarkably short—usually no more than ten or twenty lines. They focused for the most part on issues of law and public policy, for example, the need for the government to ban commercial advertising over the radio on Sundays. Only now and then did they address the subject of how Presbyterians themselves were keeping the Lord's Day.

With the onset of the Great Depression, the General Assembly began turning its attention to industrial issues, a topic it had said little about since 1920, and the progressive voice within the church was heard again, this time more forcefully and persistently than ever. In fact, from that day to this it has never been silenced. Many older progressives had supported both prohibition and the campaign to protect the Sabbath. Their aim, however, was not to privilege Presbyterian practice but to improve the condition of working people and their families. Many welcomed the New Deal reforms and were delighted with the prospect of a federal wage and hours law that would guarantee a free Sunday for most workers.

In 1931 the northern General Assembly established a special committee on social and industrial problems and charged it with investigating the great issues the Depression had brought to light and with making recommendations for what the church might do to help alleviate them. Its lengthy report, which was very progressive in tone, called for "release from employment at least one day in seven, with a shorter working week as a realizable objective" (GA, PCUSA, 1932, p. 130), but it made no mention of the Sabbath as such. The Assembly then established a new standing committee to investigate and report annually on economic issues as well as on the other social and moral issues which the church had traditionally addressed. Among these latter, of course, was the Sabbath. For a few years the new committee continued the custom of making brief and traditional statements on the Lord's Day, but in 1940, for the very first time, the Sabbath statement was given no heading of its own and was relocated within the committee report in such a way as to deemphasize its importance (GA, PCUSA, 1940, p. 179). The following year, instead of commending the Lord's Day Alliance, as was customary, the committee merely "recognized" it and asked that the denomination's relations with that organization be reexamined (GA, PCUSA, 1941, p. 169). It was a brief request, and no reasons were given. In 1942 the committee made a short Sabbath statement of a traditional nature and then turned its attention to more pressing matters.[19] Neither it nor its various successors ever concerned themselves again with the Lord's Day.

The church as a whole was also losing interest in the Sabbath. Only a handful of overtures from the lower courts were presented on the subject during the 1920s and 1930s. But in 1942 the church was still not quite ready to sever its ties with the Lord's Day Alliance or to abandon all mention of Sabbath observance.[20] The General Assembly adopted its last conventionally worded resolution on the subject—a very brief one—in 1953 (GA, PCUSA, 1953, p. 205), and the formal connection with the Lord's Day Alliance persisted for another decade, but the presbyteries and synods had dropped the Sabbath issue years earlier.

The story of the Sabbath in the northern church was not, however, entirely finished. In 1960, faced with new issues and new perspectives in the area of church-state relations, the General Assembly appointed a special committee to study the subject. Among the eleven topics the committee was asked to investigate was what posture Presbyterians should now adopt on Sunday closing laws.[21] Several important church-state cases were headed for the U.S. Supreme Court. The best remembered, of course, are the cases involving prayer and Bible reading in the public schools. But the Court had also agreed to review cases involving Sunday laws.

The committee took three years to complete its report, and when it did, it recommended that Presbyterians abandon many of their traditional claims on the state. For example, they must stop trying to censor what people can read, see, or hear (GA, UPCUSA, 1963, p. 192), and they must accept as just the recent Supreme Court decisions forbidding prayer, Bible reading, or other religious observances in the public schools (p. 186). "Moral convictions," the report declared, that are "peculiar to a religious body ought not be imposed on the general public by law."[22] In area after area, the committee asked Presbyterians to adopt positions that civil libertarians had advocated for generations. The new principle applied, of course, to Sunday laws. Presbyterians must "not seek, or even appear to seek," the committee insisted, "the coercive power of the state in order to facilitate Christians' observance of the Lord's Day" (p. 190). As for Sabbath observance, the committee affirmed "its conviction that the church itself bears sole responsibility for securing from its members a voluntary observance of the Lord's Day" (pp. 189–190). But nowhere in this report or in subsequent actions of the General Assembly was the matter of such a voluntary observance addressed.[23] In effect, the Sabbath was a dead issue among Presbyterians. The report only asked them to stop doing what most of them had already stopped doing.

The story in the southern church is different in details, but entirely the same in its outcome. The major difference is that the process took a little longer and that the General Assembly records provide a clearer view of what was going on at the grass roots. In the 1920s there was agitation in the lower courts of the southern church for reestablishing a permanent committee on the Sabbath.[24] Finally, in 1931, in the face of mounting pressure from the presbyteries, and of increasing concern for the integrity of the Lord's Day, the General Assembly did reestablish a Permanent Committee on the Sabbath, from whose many reports I have already quoted (GA, PCUS, 1931, pp. 157–158). The committee thundered away for years, and with a few exceptions its reports and recommendations were adopted by the General Assemblies.

In 1939 the committee solicited information about Sabbath observance in the church at large. It asked each minister to "talk with intelligent members of his congregation who seem lax in Sabbath observance and obtain their viewpoints, consider fully and prayerfully what is learned, reach fearless and honest conclusions," share them with his congregation, and communicate his findings to the committee (GA, PCUS, 1939, p. 117). The church ignored the committee's request. Not a single minister responded (GA, PCUS, 1940, p. 129). In 1940 the committee reissued the call (GA, PCUS, p. 130), and once again, no one responded. "The question we now have is not, What is the matter with our members?" the committee reflected, "but What is the matter with our ministers?" (GA, PCUS, 1941, p. 167). The following year, in response to an overture, the General Assembly asked each presbytery to prepare "detailed instructions for the Christian observance of the Lord's Day" and to forward them to the Presbyterian Committee of Publication for editing and distribution to the whole church (GA, PCUS, 1942, pp. 36, 93–94). Only two of the denomination's 86 presbyteries responded (GA, PCUS, 1943, p. 150), which prompted the Permanent Committee to remark that "there apparently prevails a pacific attitude and lack of militant concern on the part of a majority of our ministers, elders, deacons and members" (GA, PCUS, 1943, p. 149). Even so, for five more years the committee declaimed at length upon the subject of the Sabbath,[25] and then in 1950 the committee abruptly disappeared, a victim of a reorganization of General Assembly committees. The body charged with planning the reorganization explained that the General Assembly had far too many committees, and that "some commissioners elected or appointed to . . . minor committees felt a sense of frustration and deflated ego by being shunted to such committees." Among the "minor" committees mentioned was the Permanent Committee on the Sabbath (GA, PCUS, 1949, p. 165), which the General Assembly then proceeded to abolish, assigning its duties to an agency that would eventually become the Permanent Committee on Interchurch Relations (GA, PCUS, 1949, pp. 143, 166). No protests were recorded and no overtures on the matter were ever presented. By the end of the 1940s the bulk of Presbyterians all over the country had lost interest in the Sabbath as traditionally observed. The southern church, like the northern church, continued its affiliation with the Lord's Day Alliance for years to come,[26] and summaries of the Alliance's annual reports were duly printed in the General Assembly minutes, but on only one occasion did the Permanent Committee on Interchurch Relations issue a report of its own on Sabbath matters, and it was very brief.[27]

But a concern with Sabbath observance evidently lingered in some quarters of the southern church, for in 1957 the General Assembly concurred with an overture from the Presbytery of Potomac asking for a study of "Biblical teaching regarding the proper observance and use of the Lord's Day on the part of Christians" (GA, PCUS, 1957, pp. 30, 66). The next year the Assembly adopted the study committee's long and scholarly report, which incorporated a careful review of Old and New Testament teachings as well as some recommendations for how the Sabbath should be kept. The committee admitted that "the Day which God wanted to be a delight has become for many a dreary series of 'don'ts' " (GA, PCUS, 1958, p. 182), but instead of denouncing the church once more for its laxity, it acknowledged how hard it is "to keep the Lord's Day effectively" under modern conditions (GA, PCUS, 1958, p. 185). The committee was happy, however, to "discover in the Word of God positive guiding principles for the refreshing and fruitful uses of God's Holy Day" (GA, PCUS, 1958, p. 182). The Sabbath, it found, is a day for worship, for instruction, for rededication, for family activities, for rest, and for Christian service and rejoicing. As for family activities, the committee suggested "playing games" and "serving special refreshments" (GA, PCUS, 1958, pp. 186–187). But despite the positive and unlegalistic tone of the report, and the green light it gave to family fun on Sunday, it did not break radically with the old standards.[28] The committee did not, for example, say that it is perfectly acceptable to conduct ordinary business on Sunday. With this irenic but relatively traditional report of 1958, however, the southern church made its last formal pronouncement on the subject of how Presbyterians should observe the Sabbath.

Eleven years later, by deed rather than by word, it too announced that the Sabbath was now a dead issue.[29] In 1969 the General Assembly itself conducted regular business on Sunday. No commissioners' protests were recorded and no overtures were received on the subject. The Lord's Day Alliance was upset, but the General Assembly did not back down;[30] in fact, it continued doing business

on Sunday until its last regular meeting in 1982.[31] It too
had nothing further to say on the Sabbath. A silence had
descended on that subject that has not been broken until
this day.

A Paradigm of Decline

In my opinion, the story of the Sabbath in the twentieth
century provides a paradigm for a larger process of change
that has slowly made its way through the ranks of Presbyterians and other denominations of the old Protestant
mainline. This process involves the erosion of commitment to the churches' "old agenda" of social and spiritual
concerns. Observance of the Sabbath, including faithful
church attendance, was part of that old agenda, and so was
learning the Shorter Catechism by heart, praying and reading the Bible, refraining from worldly amusements, dress-
ing modestly, abstaining from intoxicating beverages, and
much more. Some of these items involved prohibitions,
others involved commandments; many were "hard" in the
sense of requiring a high level of commitment. What has
been happening is a process of *de*-commitment to the old
agenda items, of *de*-energization within the ranks of the
church. Moreover, when viewed over a span of decades, it
is clear that the process has been a genuinely popular one.
It is not a matter of denominational leaders putting pressure on the rank and file to drink wine or to shop on Sunday. The processes affect the rank and file as fully as they
affect the leadership. The retreat from the old positions has
sometimes produced consternation, as is evident in the
frantic statements on Sabbath desecration quoted above.
But it has never produced polarization and in some cases
has proceeded with virtually no discussion at all.

Two more generalizations may be made about this process of change. First, it has not occurred simultaneously on
all fronts but rather in a series of waves, with changes A
and B taking place before changes C and D are evident,
and changes C and D occurring before E and F. The concern with worldly amusements and modest dress was a

victim of the First World War and the 1920s. The prohibition on birth control was a victim of the 1930s and 1940s, and the strictures against drinking were victims of the 1940s and 1950s. We have already seen that the traditional Sabbath was in effect "killed off" in the 1930s and 1940s.[32] By the 1950s the Presbyterian Church was a relatively undemanding place to be, an attractive spot for people who were repelled by the stern do's and don'ts of their own upbringing, but who still wanted a Christian home base for themselves and their children.

Second, I believe that further study will show that each of these waves of change was spearheaded by a new generation of better-educated, more critical, more self-directed young adults who were unwilling to abide by the commands and prohibitions of the past without compelling new reasons or inspirations, which their elders and mentors were unable to supply. This is what the Sabbath committee was telling the southern General Assembly in 1939, and it has the ring of truth. If this process of the rebellion of younger cohorts against now this and now that element of the tradition is indeed part of the dynamic of change at the Protestant grass roots in our century, then we have yet another perspective on the threat to their very existence that the churches of the old mainline are now facing. This perspective suggests that even if there had never been a postwar baby boom or a counterculture, the churches would have begun losing their youth anyway. The losses might have been smaller and begun later, but the decline itself was simply the next step in a long process of erosion of commitment to the religious tradition. In short, it was a step whose time had come. When the distinctive elements of a tradition have eroded away, there is nothing left to discard than the shell of the tradition itself.

Religious traditions can revitalize themselves. Presbyterianism and the old Protestant mainline have done so on several occasions in the past. In fact, during much of this century a growing number of denominational leaders have tried to mobilize Christians in support of a bold new agenda of social concerns centering around peace and justice. In the process, however, they, like the rest of the church, yielded to the secularizing pressures in the culture at large that were eating away the very resources needed to restore and redirect the energies of the faithful. They, too, were embarrassed by the negative image the churches had acquired in secular circles. Moreover, in their view, what one did about civil rights or oppression in El Salvador was infinitely more important than how one spent Sunday afternoon, how often one prayed, or whom one slept with. The problem is that for the most part their new agenda did not generate enthusiasm at the grass roots. At that level of the church the main process has been one of abandoning the old agenda without embracing the new.

Which brings us back again to Sunday. Sunday *is* a trivial thing when it is weighed against the requirements of justice in southern Africa. But it is not a trivial thing when we remind ourselves that spiritual practice[33] is one of the three pillars of a religious tradition, the other two being its teachings and its morality. Spiritual practice waters the roots of the soul and thereby enlivens the spirit. When done by the members of a community, it recreates the energy to sustain its morality, which means that it is able to sustain both itself and its various missions. Without teaching and spiritual practice the will to live by the moral code of a faith fades away.

Those in the old mainline churches who want to build a world of justice and peace have no problem defining morality, or at least a morality for public affairs. But there is uncertainty in the churches on the matter of teaching, and there is a serious neglect of spirituality. The church's mission, whatever it is, cannot continue without the energy generated by its teachings and its spiritual practice. Evangelism cannot be effective if the churches have no message to proclaim that is compelling and distinctive, and no regimen for spiritual care and renewal.

The observance of Sunday was a regimen of this sort. It is out of the question to go back to the way Presbyterians observed the Sabbath in 1870, just as it is out of the question to ask that K-Mart close its doors on Sundays. But if

Presbyterians are serious about revitalization, they need to say something about sacred time and how it should be used, something about the disciplines of personal life, and something about how these matters should figure in the life of the church. The erosion of Sabbath observance is not only a paradigm of the erosion of faith in general, it is also a paradigm of the loss of spiritual practice in the mainline churches. Presbyterians dropped some important subjects years ago without saying why. If the church is to revitalize itself for whatever missions it adopts, these subjects need to be raised once again.

5

Identity and Integration: Black Presbyterians and Their Allies in the Twentieth Century

Gayraud S. Wilmore

There is a statement by Vincent Harding that accurately describes the condition in which we Blacks have found ourselves since our introduction to American Christianity in the seventeenth century:

> Indeed, one might say with confidence that whatever its other sources, the ideology of Blackness surely grows out of the deep ambivalence of American Negroes to the Christ we have encountered here. This ambivalence is not new. For we first met the American Christ on slave ships. We heard his name sung in hymns of praise while we died in our thousands, chained in stinking holds beneath the decks. . . . When our women were raped in the cabins they must have noticed the great and holy books on the shelves. Our introduction to this Christ was not propitious.[1]

I would submit that the "deep ambivalence" of which Harding speaks is not as much about Jesus Christ as it is about the white Christian church. My thesis for this essay rests upon this critical modification of Harding's observation. I have come to the tentative conclusion that since the 1890s, if not earlier, the prevailing attitude among Black members of the Presbyterian Church toward this predominantly white, middle-class denomination has been deep and persistent ambivalence. Throughout the twentieth century Black Presbyterians have oscillated back and forth between a desire for African American cultural identity and a desire for racial integration as an indispensable characteristic of any church that is truly Christian and visibly united.

Ambiguity denotes uncertainty, lacking clarity and definiteness. Ambivalence, on the other hand, denotes double-mindedness and conflict, but not necessarily confusion. Ambivalence frequently tolerates the coexistence of opposite points of view without befuddlement and mystification. Within Black Presbyterianism these two positions—racial and cultural identity and racial integration—while frequently conflictual and contradictory, have actually reinforced each other on the way to liberation and reconciliation within one inclusive and united church. In any case, it appears that a certain ambivalence has been necessary, if most Black members were to remain all these years within the folds of American Presbyterianism.

Of course, Blacks have not held ethnic self-consciousness and total assimilation in tension without the cooperation of sympathetic allies. Over the years many white Presbyterians, know and unknown, have been associated with us in the struggle. It is necessary, however, to differentiate between friends or associates and allies. Not all white liberals who have been friends have also been allies. Perhaps the major qualification for being considered an ally of the Black movement is to have somehow understood, empathized with, and supported this ambivalence, even when convinced that Black consciousness sometimes impeded what white liberals believed to be best for the struggle against American racism and oppression.

Another conclusion of my study is that not only is it possible to hold identity and integration in a creative tension, but some subtle combination of the two positions is likely to be needed as this church moves into the twenty-first century. As Presbyterians of the recently reunited church seek to explore the values and benefits of diversity-within-unity perhaps the historic ambivalence of African Americans will prove to be one of the most important contributions to the denomination's ability to survive the twentieth century and demonstrate in the twenty-first what true pluralism looks like and is able to achieve in a truly united church.

Black Presbyterians Organize
for Racial Identity and Elevation

On September 27, 1894, a small group of Black Presbyterian clergy and laity gathered at the First African Presbyterian Church of Philadelphia to form the Afro-American Presbyterian Council (AAPC)[2]. This was not the first time Black Presbyterians had caucused, for as early as 1857 their clergy had regular meetings with Black Congregational clergy to address matters of common concern.[3] Read in terms of the militant nationalism of Black Presbyterians United (BPU) in the 1960s, the statements of the Afro-American Presbyterian Council in 1894 sound strangely benign. In 1934, on the occasion of the fortieth anniversary of the Afro-American Presbyterian Council, John W. Lee, D.D., at that time pastor of the First African Presbyterian Church of Philadelphia, spelled out the reason for this second Black caucus.[4]

> The purpose for which the Council was organized was the mutual fellowship of the ministers and the churches of our group along religious, moral and social lines, who, by reason of our relation to white Presbyteries in the North, were deprived of those helpful privileges which our group enjoyed in the Southern section of the country through their own Presbyteries and Synods, where they constitute the entire body.[5]

A major concern of the Council was the lack of influence in the judicatories of the North and West compared with the power Blacks exercised in the four segregated synods of the South. What the northerners yearned for was the power to participate in the church on an equal footing with whites. It does not appear, however, that political considerations predominated in the decision to form a Black caucus in 1894. In keeping with the mood of the era of Booker T. Washington, the primary purpose of the AAPC seems to have been the cultivation of Afro-American unity and racial advancement. It was assumed that both required a certain freedom from white control. The overarching concern of most Blacks in both major divisions of Presbyterianism was to elevate themselves through racial self-help, solidarity, and identity. This is not to suggest that all of the organizers of the Council were followers of Booker T. Washington. Actually the early AAPC was staunchly opposed to Washington's position of racial accommodation, but there was no impulse to become a political pressure group for racial integration either. Basically conservative in their theology and genteel in their methods of pursuing individual and collective goals, these elite Black Calvinists of the early twentieth century sought to prove their worth to both friends and detractors by their demonstrable intelligence, middle-class life-style, and moralistic values.

It is no accident that the idea for creating a national American Negro Academy, an organization for intellectual and cultural elevation, was conceived the year before the AAPC was founded. The principal architects of this famous Academy were two distinguished clergymen, Francis J. Grimké, pastor of the Fifteenth Street Presbyterian Church in Washington, D.C., and Alexander Crummell, rector of St. Luke's Episcopal Church in Washington and perhaps the most celebrated Black churchman in the nation at the time.[6] The interests of the two movements—the ANA and the AAPC—parallel each other across the turn of the century and show many similarities. Much of the elitism of the American Negro Academy is reflected in some of the papers and addresses of the annual meetings of the AAPC, of which Grimké served as the second president.[7] It is significant that among the early members of the Academy were no less than four highly esteemed and influential Black Presbyterian clergymen: John B. Reeves, pastor of the Central Presbyterian Church of Philadelphia and former head of the theological department of Howard University, Daniel J. Sanders, the first Black president of Biddle Institute (later to become Johnson C. Smith University), Matthew Anderson, pastor of Berean Presbyterian Church in Philadelphia, and Francis J. Grimké, pastor of the Fifteenth Street Presbyterian Church in Washington, D.C.[8] More than any of the others, Grimké and Anderson, who were towering figures in both the ANA and the AAPC, illustrate the complex relationship among members of the AAPC between middle-class proprieties and Black religion, voluntary segregation and pressure politics, ethnic identity and the desire for integration.

Grimké was the most influential in the early days of the caucus. The son of a Black slave woman and a white planter of South Carolina, educated at Lincoln University, in Pennsylvania, and at Princeton Theological Seminary, a distinguished preacher and lecturer, he fought bitterly against the proposed union with the southern church in 1888 and against union with the Cumberland Presbyterian Church in 1905.[9] At the same time he expressed serious doubts about the commitment of white Presbyterians in the North to racial equality.[10] Although he was a member of the anti-Bookerite faction of the Black clergy, Grimké was by no means a radical Black nationalist. Indeed, according to the testimony of a contemporary who knew him well, he kept a certain distance and aloofness from the caucus he had helped to bring into existence.[11] Like W. E. B. Du Bois, with whom he worked to create the Niagara Movement—the predecessor of the NAACP—Grimké combined pride of race and a deep concern for Black history and culture with a fierce moral integrity and sense of fair play. Throughout his life he refused to compromise with segregation. But like Du Bois, and unlike his fellow Presbyterian Matthew Anderson, Grimké seems to have lacked that common touch which would enable him to associate with ordinary folk. Such identity with the Black lower class might mean, and often did mean, postponing justice due from whites for the sake of operational unity among Blacks.

Regional and Denominational Differences
Between Black Presbyterians

For most of the first half of the twentieth century Black Presbyterians in the North and South were out of touch with each other. They had, to some extent, different perspectives on an appropriate posture for African Americans in the two major Presbyterian bodies. In North and South Carolina and Georgia men like Daniel J. Sanders; Albert M. McCoy, successor to John M. Gaston, Secretary of the Unit of Work for Colored People of the Board of National Missions of the Presbyterian Church U.S.A. (referred to here as the northern church); William L. Metz, a highly respected pastor on Edisto Island; Henry L. McCrorey, Dean of Johnson C. Smith Seminary; A. H. Prince and Frank C. Shirley, field representatives for Atlantic and Catawba Synods, were forced by the circumstances under which they labored to make necessary adjustments to the restrictive policies of the South.[12] Although they were ministers of the northern church, these men accepted the "separate but equal" dictum of *Plessy v. Ferguson* as applicable to the church as well as to the society.

Moreover, at the end of the nineteenth century it was the intention of the Presbyterian Church U.S. (referred to as the southern church) to actually separate the races in two denominations. Between 1898 and 1916 an independent Afro-American Presbyterian Church was created by the southern church. It was only brought back into that denomination as the Snedecor Memorial Synod when it proved too weak to make it on its own.[13] Until the 1950s the segregated Presbyterian, U.S., Synod of Snedecor and the equally segregated Presbyterian, U.S.A., Synods of Catawba, Atlantic, Canadian, and Blue Ridge represented Black Presbyterian power in the South, unrivaled by anything comparable in the northern-based Afro-American Presbyterian Council or its successor caucuses. It is true, nevertheless, that the ecclesiastical power that the Black judicatories enjoyed at the General Assembly level did not protect them or their congregations from the onerous paternalism that both white Presbyterian churches carried over into the twentieth century from their missionary activity among the freed people during the Reconstruction.

Bryant George, formerly of the mission strategy staff of the UPCUSA Board of National Missions and an astute observer of the power alignments of the church in the Southeast, tells how Dr. John M. Gaston, who joined the Board of Missions for Freedmen in 1910 and for nearly three decades directed the northern church's work with Blacks, maintained a private residence on the campus of Johnson C. Smith University. Gaston kept a close eye and tight rein on the Black churches by commuting back and forth between Charlotte and Pittsburgh, where the purse strings of the mission programs were held. Gaston was from the old school and enjoyed all the deferences and privileges of a plantation manager before the Unit for Colored Work was finally dissolved in 1938.[14] It is not difficult to imagine why Black Presbyterians in the North wanted at all costs to avoid the tender mercies of the Freedmen's Board. Thomas J. B. Harris, for many years the executive of the AAPC and presently residing in Englewood, New Jersey, at 103 years old, says that one of the primary reasons for the foundation of the Council was to prevent Black churches in the North from being patronized by the national boards and agencies.[15] In an address before the 128th General Assembly, meeting in Atlantic City in 1916, Matthew Anderson spoke for the entire AAPC when he said:

> I express the unanimous sentiments of the ministry and the intelligent laity of the colored Presbyterians in the north when I say that we do not want any special ecclesiastical legislation for our churches, nor special Boards for their supervision and direction; we must stand precisely where the white churches stand, having the same rights and privileges, absolutely the same status, if we would be Presbyterians. For this reason, therefore, we are not willing to be placed arbitrarily under the Freedmen's Board or any other Board gotten up specially to manage colored work.[16]

Throughout this period the relationship was strained between Blacks in the North and those in the four segregated synods of the South, not to mention between both of those groups and Blacks in the Presbyterian Church U.S. and the Second Cumberland Presbyterian Church. Class and perhaps even color differences were exacerbated by this lack of communication and by the disinclination of the northern clergy to be drawn into the orbit of the Board of Freedmen. It was not until after the consolidation of several agencies of the Presbyterian Church U.S.A. into the Board of National Missions in 1923, bringing work with Blacks in both regions into one Division of Missions for Colored People, that the feeling of estrangement began to dissipate.

During the next decade the Council, with its name changed to the Afro-American Presbyterian Council of the North and West, with four regional directors to "supervise, encourage, develop and extend the interest of the Churches in their areas," received fraternal delegates from the four Black synods at its annual meetings and attempted to present a united Afro-American front to the denomination.[17] Already by 1934 it was meeting regularly with national staff people to advise and coordinate the work with Black congregations. Thus, a subtle change in orientation occurred among Blacks in the northern church between the wars. As the Andersons, Reeveses, and Grimkés of the earlier period passed from the scene, Black Presbyterians began to shift from elitist racial identity emphases. They took a greater interest in church growth and institutional development, pressing the denomination for Black staff and committee appointments. They sought increased funds to help their churches become self-supporting, and they gave more attention to racial integration in all aspects of Presbyterian life and work. With the retirement of Gaston in 1938, the change of the title of the Unit of Work *for* Colored People, to the Unit of Work *with* Colored People, and the appointment of Albert B. McCoy, the first Black to serve as a Board executive in the denomination, a new era began. Elitist solidarity and cultural identity concerns became increasingly subordinated to the widely accepted goal of racial integration.

By 1947 the Council issued a public statement.

The Afro-American Presbyterian Council is definitely a movement of interim strategy. The council has never entertained the idea of setting up a segregated group within the Presbyterian church. It has no brief to support a perpetuation of local Negro churches, nor does it desire or intend to become a pressure group within the church. Nevertheless, the council takes the strongest stand against segregation everywhere and in every form. . . . The sum total of the council's aims and objectives is to help the church to become a truly inclusive fellowship.[18]

If Anderson and Grimké typified Black Presbyterian leadership before World War I, Albert B. McCoy and George Lake Imes, the latter a field representative appointed by the Boards of National Missions and Christian Education in 1945 to serve as liaison between themselves and the Council of the North and West, typify the leadership in the interim between the Great Depression and the critical years of the 1950s and 1960s. The decades of the 1940s and 1950s called for the special talents of Black bureaucrats who could fill the vacuum left by the Freedmen's Board and the white-led Negro work of the newly consolidated Boards of National Missions and Christian Education. What was initially a white paternalism rapidly became a Black paternalism under white supervision. National Missions funds designated as salary supplements continued to be used to hold rebellious ministers and their churches in line with the conservative policies of New York and Philadelphia. This was particularly true in the case of the Synods of Catawba and Atlantic. Some of the younger clergy complained that Dr. McCoy and later Dr. Jesse B. Barber, who assumed the office upon McCoy's death in 1951, were veritable dictators who held the allocations of the mission program in trust for the "Great White Fathers and Brethren" of the northern church. This may be an unfair judgment upon several men and women who were appointed to staff positions between 1938 and 1958, but it is certain that the commission given to a few Blacks to lead others had implicit reservations built in and was never intended to supersede the prerogatives of middle judicatories and a General Assembly that repeatedly rejected the petitions of the AAPC and had neglected the nonwhite constituencies of the denomination during most of the century.

Black Presbyterians in the Era of Desegregation

The Presbyterian Historical Society in Philadelphia has preserved a memorandum sent by Rev. John Dillingham, pastor of the 13th Avenue Presbyterian Church in Newark, New Jersey, to Rev. L. Charles Gray of the Lafayette Church in Jersey City, dated November 19, 1953, that sets the stage for the dissolution of the Afro-American Council of the North and West in 1957. Dillingham spoke for some key Black Presbyterian clergy of the time when he wrote:

> From the time I first joined the Council in 1940 to the present, I have always looked upon it as an unfortunate, though NECESSARY organization. Being a southerner by birth, I have been rather sensitive about conditions that suggest segregation. I have cooperated with the Council, however, because I recognized that we faced certain facts and not just theories. Moreover, I interpreted our role as being that of "working ourselves out of a job". . . . New occasions, however, do teach new duties and time makes ancient good uncouth. The higher judicatories of our Church in the North and West are recognizing Negroes and electing them as Commissioners. In Synods like New Jersey, all ministers and elders in the Synoa may attend its annual meeting. Furthermore, Negroes are being recognized in presbyteries not only as members of important Committees, but also as moderators (Detroit, Philadelphia, etc.) One Negro also has served as moderator of the Synod of California and Nevada.[19]

In this memo Dillingham alludes to an important action of the National Council of Churches in 1946 which was aaopted and made its own by the General Assembly of the northern church—the famous call for "a non-segregatea church in a non-segregated society." This action, more than any other prior to the civil rights movement of the 1960s, impelled the church toward the goal of desegregation.

Dillingham was impressed. "If General Assembly," he writes, "will go so far as to adopt a resolution calling for the dissolution of Negro Synods and Presbyteries as submitted by the Standing Committee on Social Education and Action at the 165th Assembly, then it is high time for us to rethink the place and function of the Council." Dillingham went on to recommend that the Council should go further to renounce racial identity.

> To implement this ideal, it might be necessary to change our name again just as it was changed from "Afro-American Presbyterian Council" to "Presbyterian Council in the North and West." The new name should reflect not only a change in emphasis, but also the fact that we are talking about a United Church today.[20]

The Dillingham proposal was never implemented. But in 1957, in the glow of an unprecedented era of good feeling—largely generated by Clifford Earle, Margaret Kuhn, and other white allies in the national program of Social Education and Action of the Board of Christian Education—the Council voluntarily voted itself out of existence. Almost everyone was satisfied with this surprising turn of affairs, but some clergy and laity felt that the action was premature and excessively optimistic about the demise of racism in the Presbyterian Church. Leroy Patrick, who at that time pastored Fifth Church in Chester, Pennsylvania, makes the following comment about those heady days:

> We—all of us—were in a state of euphoria, a shameful confession for those to make who had studied under Niebuhr The Supreme Court had spoken. The Church's pronouncements were unequivocal. Freedom had finally arrived. Segregation's death knell had been sounded. Discrimination was over. Away with our little black organization. We would miss the fun, the fellowship, the camaraderie, but we had to give ourselves to the New Day.[21]

Two of the persons who readily conceded that a grave error had been made were Elo L. Henderson, the founder and pastor of the Grier Heights Church in Charlotte, elected in 1955 as the executive of the Synod of Catawba, and Edler G. Hawkins, a past president of the Council and founder and pastor of St. Augustine Presbyterian Church in the Bronx. Henderson in the South and Hawkins in the North represented a new, militant posture for Black Presbyterians so recently beguiled and pacified by the attitudinal-change approach to race relations that came out of the Board of Christian Education prior to Clifford Earle, Margaret Kuhn, and H. Ben Sissel. A third Black leader came to the fore in the southern church, but with a somewhat different orientation. Lawrence W. Bottoms, perhaps the best known Black minister in the Presbyterian Church U.S., joined Alex R. Batchelor as Assistant Secretary of the Division of Negro Work in 1951. Although the social action wing of the southern Presbyterian church, comparable to Social Education and Action in the northern church, introduced the policy changes of the 1950s, Dr. Bottoms initiated an emphasis on Black new church development that brought the first leap in the membership of Black Presbyterians in the Presbyterian Church U.S. from approximately 3,000 in 1949 to almost 7,000 in 1958.[22] The increasing sensitivity of southern Presbyterians to the demands of the 1950s and 1960s was due in part to this infusion from the Black urban middle class as a result of Bottoms' style of leadership, which was based on his conviction that "brotherhood is deeper than a political issue, it is a moral issue."[23] His position rarely failed to get a respectable hearing in conservative Presbyterian, U.S., circles where the "spirituality of the church" was a major theological tenet. In the meantime, many white clergy and laity in both branches of Presbyterianism had changed during the decade of the 1950s. In the South the change was massive. Ernest Trice Thompson analyzes what was happening among southern Presbyterians during this period.

> A number of factors led them to reassess their Christian obligation; among them a second world war in which Negroes fought for a country which denied them first-class citizenship, the mood of the returning soldiers, the Fair Employment Practice Commission (FEPC) of the war years, the drive for civil rights, the stepped-up activity of the NAACP, a series of court decisions admitting Negroes to institutions

of higher learning and threatening segregating education in
the public schools.[24]

But it was in 1954, just prior to the Supreme Court decision in the Brown case, that the Council of Christian Relations grasped the nettle. The church then affirmed that
"enforced segregation of the races is discrimination which
is out of harmony with Christian theology and ethics." At
the forefront of this development were people like Mal-
colm Calhoun, John Marion, Aubrey Brown, Rachel
Henderlite, and later, George Chauncey of the Division of
Christian Relations. Joseph L. Roberts, a Black northern
Presbyterian minister who joined the staff of the Board of
National Ministries in 1970 to begin the new unit on Corporate and Social Missions, says that by that time "there
were thirty to forty southern Presbyterian allies in pastor-
ates and on the national staffs who could be depended
upon to put their bodies where their mouths were on the
issue of racial justice."[25]

In 1947 William H. McConaghy, a white minister from
Albany, New York, and Jesse B. Barber, from Lincoln University, were selected by the northern church to set up a
new Institute on Racial and Cultural Relations, which became the rallying point for white allies.[26] During the 1950s
these friends and allies tended to coalesce around the Department of Social Education and Action of the Board of
Christian Education and the program of urban and industrial work of the Board of National Missions. With the
election of William A. Morrison and Kenneth G. Neigh as
General Secretaries of the Boards of Christian Education
and National Missions respectively, a new day dawned for
race relations in the United Presbyterian Church U.S.A.
With the cooperation of John C. Smith, General Secretary
of the Commission on Ecumenical Mission and Relations,
and Eugene Carson Blake, Stated Clerk of the General Assembly, who had been carefully educated to the realities
of Black-white relations by Edler Hawkins and other
members of the Black caucus, the three program boards
launched the Commission on Religion and Race (CORAR)

in 1963. Thus, the United Presbyterians became the first national denomination to respond with a Black-led staff and a generous program budget to the civil rights movement of Dr. Martin Luther King, Jr., and must be given major credit for catalyzing the policy decisions and funds that produced the first Commission on Religion and Race in the National Council of Churches earlier that year.[27]

It is important to mention that during this period many Black Presbyterian women came to the forefront of the struggle for equality in the church. One thinks particularly of Emily Gibbes, Gladys Cole, Mildred Artis, Evelyn Gordon, Mildred Davis, Thelma Adair, and Mary Jane Patterson, to mention a few. Of course, from the early days of the Afro-American Presbyterian Council women played a critical role as presenters of papers and leaders of discussion groups on education, the Black family, and youth activities. At the beginning of this century most of the female leaders were the wives of ministers, many well-educated and talented in their own right. But by the 1940s and 1950s other church women began to take their places at the annual meetings of the AAPC, the summer conferences at Lincoln University, near Oxford, Pennsylvania, and the popular "Workers Conferences" that convened each summer at Johnson C. Smith University in Charlotte, North Carolina. It would not be an exaggeration to say that without the leadership of extraordinarily gifted women the National Black Presbyterian Caucus of today would not exist.

Black Presbyterian Militance
During the Civil Rights Period

The ferment that led to the creation of new caucuses within both Presbyterian churches began in the United Presbyterian Church U.S.A. with the organization of what was called Concerned Presbyterians by Bryant George and Edler Hawkins in 1963. This new group was not patterned after the old Council of the North and West. It was unabashedly political and played a key role in the campaign Bryant George managed which helped to elect Edler G.

Hawkins Moderator of the 176th General Assembly in 1964—the year after the caucus was founded, essentially for that purpose. Having lost by two votes to Herman Turner of Atlanta at the Des Moines Assembly in 1963, Edler Hawkins, with strong interracial lobbying across the church for a year, was finally elected the first Black Moderator at Oklahoma City the next year.

It is not possible to discuss here the role of the Commission on Religion and Race, which under a new mandate in 1968 became the Council on Church and Race (COCAR) and the most impressive achievement of Black Presbyterians and their allies in the 1960s. Both Presbyterian churches established Councils on Church and Race in the 1960s and 1970s, and these programs, staffed by Blacks and strongly supported by Black and white caucuses outside the official structures, represent the apex of Presbyterian involvement in racial justice issues during the most difficult years of the civil rights movement. In the northern church the ground was prepared for the Commission on Religion and Race by the Committee of Eighteen of the Board of Christian Education, which included the always dignified but irrepressible Edler Hawkins, and the reconstitution of the old Council of the North and West as the Concerned Presbyterians (note the absence of any racial designation in the name) in 1963.[28]

In the southern church the Council on Church and Race was preceded by the strategic appointment to the national staff in 1970 of Joseph L. Roberts, a Black UPCUSA pastor from New Jersey. It is significant, however, that Roberts' appointment was preceded by the creation of the Black Presbyterian Leadership Caucus of the PCUS in 1969.[29] In both instances it is doubtful that anything would have happened without aggressive Black caucusing, or without the support of white allies both within and outside the boards and agencies.[30]

The same year that Concerned Presbyterians recaptured the initiative of Blacks for increased visibility and power in the United Presbyterian Church U.S.A., a new interracial caucus was founded that was to become a major source of white support during the 1960s and 1970s. On May 16, 1963, a group of Black and white commissioners and visitors to the Des Moines Assembly came together to form a "mass membership organization" that called itself the Presbyterian Interracial Council (PIC). Its purpose was to recruit individuals for direct action work in the civil rights movement in behalf of the UPCUSA, to "identify with and work directly and openly with Negro and other minority groups in a persistent daring witness to minority communities," and to "give timely attention to immediate local and national issues whenever and wherever trouble breaks out."[31] Headquartered in Chicago under the leadership of Kenneth Waterman, its first Executive Secretary, PIC had more than a thousand members organized in twelve local chapters by the end of its first year.[32] It was undoubtedly one of the most successful programs in race relations ever launched by Presbyterians. PIC played a critical role in electing Hawkins to the office of Moderator at the 176th General Assembly. Its local chapters educated white Presbyterians on the etiquette of race relations at a time when few had any association with Blacks. Members of PIC chapters worked on fair housing programs, formed voting blocs that helped to get supportive policies adopted by presbyteries and synods, and recruited Presbyterian and other clergy for participation in the CORAR direct action project in Hattiesburg, Mississippi. PIC also cooperated with the Council on Church and Race in various relief efforts during the northern city rebellions between 1964 and 1968.[33]

The Dream of Integration Unfulfilled

A relevant question at this point in our discussion is: Why, at the highest point of United Presbyterian participation in the civil rights movement, which saw CORAR and PIC created in 1963 and Hawkins elected Moderator in 1964, was an unbreakable seal not cemented between Black and white Presbyterians, with the consequence of the truly integrated church that was the goal of the Council of the North and West and the reason for its admittedly premature dissolution in 1957?

The answer is complex. Obviously, the efforts made between 1963 and 1973 were not sufficient to make up for more than two hundred years of segregation and paternalism in both churches. Despite the historic contribution of the northern church to Black education in the South after the Civil War, its post-World War II sponsorship of aggressive community organization, urban ministries, and the civil rights movement, and its integration of several important staff and committee positions in the national church and lower judicatories, Presbyterians continue to be an overwhelmingly white denomination with Blacks greatly underrepresented in proportion to their numbers in American Protestantism. Black Presbyterian congregations are still small and are generally unable to remain integrated where they have evolved from previously white congregations in changing neighborhoods. Although some downtown and suburban churches have received Black members without difficulty, the price of amicable relations has usually required that African Americans divest themselves of any conspicuous cultural Blackness and become quietly assimilated to a white, middle-class milieu. Almost no healthy white congregations have called Black pastors, and the Black masses, on the whole, have not been attracted even to all-Black Presbyterian congregations in the numbers in which they have been drawn since the turn of the century to Baptist, Methodist, Pentecostal, or even Roman Catholic churches.

Another answer to the question about the failure of full-scale integration in the Presbyterian Church has to do with internal contradictions between racial integration and ethnic identity. If the ambivalence of Black Presbyterians toward the white church requires a strong interracial caucus as well as a strong Black caucus, it is certain that we have not yet learned how to manage both at the same time. A study of the activity of the Presbyterian Interracial Council will show that it began to decline as Black Presbyterians United (BPU), the new Black caucus established in the northern church in 1968, became more politically active on the presbytery level and more successful in forcing the church to recognize and appreciate the African American cultural heritage on the national level.[34]

It seems evident that there has been a reciprocal relationship between the failure of the church to become fully integrated and the swing of many Black Presbyterians, disillusioned by that failure, back to cultural identity and Black consciousness in recent years. Similarly on the national scene, the call for Black Power, the founding of the National Committee of Black Churchmen in Dallas in 1967, and a new emphasis on a more Afrocentric culture, arose partly from the disappointment of the masses, particularly the youth, with the pace and quality of integration under Dr. King and the liberal coalition he had been able to put together with northern Democrats and the labor movement. But out of what was essentially a negative reaction in the ranks of mass-based organizations and community groups, a positive thrust toward Black pride and cultural nationalism developed in the late 1960s to give impetus to a movement for theological renewal in both Black Protestant circles and Black Roman Catholicism. The National Committee of Black Churchmen, the National Black Evangelical Association, the National Office of Black Catholics, the Society for the Study of Black Religion, and the Black Theology Project of Theology in the Americas were all institutional expressions of the remarkable flowering of African American theological reflection and praxis in the United States between 1964 and 1975.[35]

The Manifesto and Angela Davis Crises

The ability of Black Presbyterians in the northern church to stand together was subjected to its most stringent test less than three years after Black Presbyterians United was created in the fall of 1968, immediately following the Second Annual Convocation of the militant interdenominational caucus, the National Committee of Black Churchmen, in St. Louis, Missouri. The first test came at

the San Antonio General Assembly in 1969 when the caucus urged the church to respond favorably to the Black
Manifesto of James Forman and the Black Economic Development Conference which BPU and NCBC supported.
The Manifesto was rejected, but the demands of the caucus
for radical change did not go unheeded. The Program for
the Self-Development of People was one of the consequences of the confrontation at San Antonio.

The second test involved one of the most controversial
and least understood developments in the recent history of
American Presbyterianism—the infamous Angela Davis affair.[36] The new alliance between Black Presbyterians and
the bureaucracy of the boards and agencies of the national
church was shaken to its core by the crisis over the young
communist woman from California, but the coalition held
firm despite cries of outrage from the grass roots. With an
unprecedented flood of letters and telegrams pouring into
local church offices and to harried officials at 475 Riverside
Drive in New York City, an incensed laity mounted a well-
organized campaign to punish and possibly discharge the
Council on Church and Race at the 183rd General Assembly, meeting in Rochester, New York, in May of 1971.

In a memorable address to the Assembly, Edler Hawkins
reviewed the details of a grant of $10,000 from the Emer-
gency Fund for Legal Aid that COCAR had made to ensure that Ms. Davis would receive a fair trial. As usual,
Edler's approach was the soul of moderation, but no one at
the Assembly could mistake his gentility for the lack of will
to keep the Assembly supportive of the mandate it had
given for its racial justice agency to represent the United
Presbyterian Church on the cutting edge of the civil rights
movement.

> Our hope is that no one confuse the issue in a discussion of
> Miss Davis' political affiliation. This case was before our
> Council for help because of a legitimate appeal of a judicatory
> of the church, a Session of a local church situated in the area
> in which Miss Davis is being held, and because our mandate
> is on the basis of the implications of race, we made the grant
> because we knew this Black lady needed help in securing an

adequate defense *just* because she was Black, and a woman, and because she too, must be treated as "innocent" until proven guilty. . . . That grant for legal aid by which hundreds have been helped, is an investment in . . . the American system of justice, as an act of faith, that the rule of law, and the administration of justice in this land will be laid-on fairly and without discrimination to all Americans, be they Black, or White, Red, Yellow or Brown, or poor.[37]

The Standing Committee on Church and Race of the Rochester Assembly nervously considered the various proposals floating around the church to denounce the grant, discipline COCAR, and exonerate the denomination from the taint of communism. Many agreed with the conservative group, the Presbyterian Lay Committee, Inc., that the Legal Defense funds had been misused in the case of Angela Davis and that, in this and many other instances since its creation in 1963, the Council on Church and Race had far exceeded its mandate.[38] In its final report the Standing Committee refused to repudiate unequivocally the COCAR action. It did, however, accept from the floor amendments to its cautious recommendation that the General Assembly continue the Emergency Fund for Legal Aid under the administration of COCAR. After one of the stormiest debates in the recent history of Presbyterian General Assemblies the following motion was approved in connection with the report of the Standing Committee on Church and Race: " . . . that the 183rd General Assembly communicate to COCAR its serious question concerning the propriety of allocating $10,000 to the Marin County Black Defense Fund."

During the weeks following the Rochester Assembly it became clear that Black Presbyterian leadership across the nation was unified behind Edler Hawkins, the chairman of COCAR, and resented the way the majority of white Presbyterians had cast aspersion upon what Blacks considered to be the good judgment, patriotism, and moral integrity of the COCAR staff. As in the past, a small minority of white Presbyterians at national and regional levels and in the Presbyterian Interracial Council held the line against an onslaught of several thousand communications from people in the local congregations bemoaning the "ill-advised action" of the Council on Church and Race in giving money to "that Black communist bitch," or words of similar effect.

In a much neglected but historic document entitled "Why Angela Davis?" (prepared by the National Race Staff, an interagency secretariat coordinated by COCAR staff), an ideologically and theologically cohesive response was made to its critics. In a section that refers to the support it was receiving from the powerful office of the Stated Clerk of the General Assembly, the statement of the national staff reads in part:

> The Council on Church and Race, by recommendation of the National Race Staff and under the criteria established for the Emergency Legal Aid Fund, made the grant to the defense fund for Angela Davis *because it believed in what the United Presbyterian Church has always professed about justice, liberation and reconciliation.* There is room for honest disagreement with this decision. But as the Stated Clerk of the General Assembly, Mr. William P. Thompson has said, "It's easy for us to provide help for people who conform to our standards. It is a real test of our commitment to the principles involved if we are prepared to help those who don't conform to our standards." The Stated Clerk expressed his willingness to defend the right of members of the church to disapprove of the Council's action, but he also expressed the hope that objectors would continue to support the church. If that counsel goes unheeded by the members of this predominantly white church not only will the United Presbyterian mission suffer untold injury, but perhaps even more important, a rupture will open up in our church between black and white that may be irremediable.[39]

The fear of an irreconcilable breakdown in relations between Black and white Presbyterians was real. During the summer and fall of 1971 chapters of Black Presbyterians United fought off the criticism of friends and associates in the presbyteries by a critique of their own. BPU criticized what it regarded as the inconstancy of the church on the issue of political dissension exacerbated by the all too familiar prejudice against Black people. The question arose, shortly after the Rochester Assembly, whether BPU should take some dramatic action to communicate to the denomination at large its feeling of betrayal by what appeared to be a large scale abandonment by white Presbyterians of their previously advanced position on racial justice. When the logistics of assembling the caucus in an emergency session seemed unmanageable, Bryant George, Edler Hawkins, and Robert P. Johnson, the executive of the Presbytery of New York City, conceived the idea of returning the $10,000 at a press conference as a way of saying to the church, and particularly to the Black community across the nation, that prominent Black members were willing to do for Angela Davis what a predominantly white General Assembly regarded as an "unfortunate impropriety."

On June 15, 1971, twenty Black Presbyterian clergy and laity, the top leadership of the denomination and of BPU, were called by telephone. Within twenty-four hours each sent a check for $500.00, out of personal funds, to make it possible for the defense fund grant to be repaid to the church, thus rendering the original grant not from a reluctant white church, but from a group of unabashedly supportive and indignant Black Presbyterians. Many felt that this action was the least that could be done to vindicate the honor, independence, and fearlessness of BPU, although some of the official explanations fell short of such implications. In handing over the twenty personal checks to Kenneth G. Neigh, General Secretary of the Board of National Missions, Robert Pierre Johnson, spokesperson for the caucus, said:

> We as Black Presbyterians acknowledge publicly our distress at the outcry generated within our Church as a result of . . . the allocation of funds to guarantee a fair trial for Angela Davis. . . . We are presenting $10,000 to the Church as an affirmation of our personal commitment to justice in our land . . . at considerable sacrifice to ourselves and our families.[40]

Johnson added that what was being done that day was "an indication to the Black community that there are Black Presbyterians who are more willing to affirm the rectitude of the Church's legal aid to Angela Davis than many white Presbyterians are willing to reject that rectitude." It was obvious that some Black Presbyterians felt let down by their white allies and were embarrassed by indications that Black Presbyterians were being laughed at by Black Americans in general for being unequally yoked with racists in an overwhelmingly white church.

The issue of Black consciousness and pride had figured largely in the decision in 1968 to scrap the nondescript designation of "Concerned Presbyterians," reduce dependency on the goodwill and reconciliation strategy of the Presbyterian Interracial Council, link the fortunes of Black Presbyterians with the new National Committee of Black Churchmen (later to become the National Conference of Black Christians), and create a Black caucus in the church that white power was bound to respect. Edler Hawkins and several other seasoned activists agreed in St. Louis to recede into the background and permit a younger, more militant leadership to come forward. E. Wellington Butts, the young pastor of Bethany Presbyterian Church in Englewood, New Jersey, was elected the first BPU president, but Edler Hawkins, the chairman of the dissolved Concerned Presbyterians and the Commission on Church and Race, could not avoid being regarded as the spiritual father and mentor of the new caucus. Since the Council of the North and West and PIC had both emphasized integration, a theological and psychological adjustment had to be made by many of the pastors and lay leaders who gravitated to BPU. But younger leaders like Butts, Eugene Turner, and J. Oscar McCloud had no recollection of the policies of men like Dillingham, Leroy Patrick, and L. Charles Gray. They were much more attuned to the Black Power movement tactics of the Student Nonviolent Coordinating Committee and the National Committee of Black Churchmen, that is, to Black consciousness and Black theology. A new style of leadership—reminiscent of Francis J. Grimké,

but even more of Matthew Anderson, John B. Reeves, and
Reuben H. Armstrong—developed around Edler Hawkins
and the younger churchmen who revered him. Throughout
the years between 1963, when he came into national prom-
inence, and his death in 1977, Hawkins had skillfully held
in tension the twin goals of Black cultural identity and
interracial integration.

Radicalization and Reconciliation

The Angela Davis affair radicalized Hawkins and other
Black Presbyterians even more than the Black Manifesto
crisis of 1969, which left them disappointed by the evasive
response of the denomination to the demand for reparations. At no time, however, did they reject its compromise
of agreeing to release certain National Missions properties
for economic development in the South and creating the
Program for the Self-Development of People.[41] Actually
Edler Hawkins kept a balanced perspective about the interracial character of the Presbyterian Church through the
years. The battles with conservative whites over the Black
Manifesto and the Emergency Legal Defense Fund never
blunted his sensitivity to the need for white allies in the
struggle for justice and reconciliation between the races in
both the church and the society.

In the fall of 1963 Hawkins received a letter from a former seminary classmate asking whether or not there was a
place for white liberals in the movement. His response,
warm and engaging as always, yet insistent on the point
that there was still a need for Blacks to keep the pressure
on through their own organizations, shows how he walked
the fine line between Black radicalism and reconciliation
with whites. After presenting the position of Black leadership dismayed by a report that six out of every ten northern whites believed that Blacks were being treated "about
right," or "too well," Hawkins concluded his letter by expressing disagreement with radical opinion on both sides.
He then sought to reassure his white friend about the desir-
ability of interracial coalitions.

Let no doubts disturb you in the days ahead as to whether you are needed, for despite the oft repeated feeling on the part of the Negro personality that his freedom will never come apart from his own involvement and leadership, it can never really be assured until the true liberal helps to prepare white America in all ways that he can, for the urgent business of civil rights that is the business of all America.[42]

The Black leadership of the United Presbyterian Church U.S.A. adopted one of the most radical strategies among the ethnic caucuses that came out of the civil rights movement. It constantly pressed the white constituency to recognize the necessity of the Black consciousness movement. But Black Presbyterians never espoused a doctrine of separatism. Rather they understood Black pride, solidarity, and the sharing of power with whites as both desirable and indispensable for racial justice and reconciliation in the United States and in South Africa.

The role of Edler G. Hawkins in both Black Presbyterians United and in the Presbyterian Interracial Council is a classic example of the creative ambivalence Vincent Harding wrote about in his insightful essay on "Black Power and the American Christ." One hopes that the appropriation of this heritage will neither impede the movement toward the one holy catholic and apostolic church of the great creeds, nor the empirical church in which every group finds its history and culture acknowledged, appreciated, and used for the benefit of all.[43] It remains for the present generation of Black Presbyterians and their allies to help the reunited church discover a reconciling inclusiveness that makes use of the African American cultural inheritance, and other ethnic inheritances, without dividing us up into warring camps that will destroy everything for which the faithful men and women, of every race and nationality who preceded us, struggled and prayed.

6

Ministry of Word and Sacrament: Women and Changing Understandings of Ordination

Barbara Brown Zikmund

During a recent sabbatical, I did research at the Schlesinger Library of Women's History at Radcliffe College and rented a room at the Episcopal Divinity School in Cambridge, Massachusetts. It was very interesting to be living in the midst of an Episcopal community when they celebrated the consecration of the first woman bishop in the history of Anglicanism, the Right Reverend Barbara Clementine Harris. The question of orders and ordination, the views of clergy and laity, the situation of women in church and society all became more visible in Boston on February 11, 1989. As the *New York Times* put it, "The service broke a barrier for all the major branches of Christianity that recognize that bishops have a divinely mandated authority as successors to Jesus' apostles."[1] The consecration of a female bishop, which conservatives denounced as a "sacrilegious imposture," stands at the end of a historical development which has increasingly recognized the legitimacy of women's leadership in the church. It is this development that I want to examine.

What Is Ordination?

Historically, the setting apart of certain persons by prayer and laying on of hands to the ministry of Word and sacrament goes back to the biblical period. The exercise of the ministry of the church has taken many different forms in the course of history. As understandings of spirituality, church, society, and world change, so do theologies of ministry.[2] I am convinced that the changing role of women in our times is providing another challenge and critique of ministry as it has been identified with ordination.

What is ordination? Why has the church developed and sustained the practice of "setting apart" certain persons by prayer and the laying on of hands to the ministry of Jesus Christ? What does that mean to the church and to the individual who becomes ordained?

Generally speaking, although many texts discuss the ministry of the early Christian community, there are only four biblical texts that refer specifically to the act of laying on hands that we associate with ordination.[3]

In Acts we read that the Twelve said to the gathered Christians, "Pick out from among you seven men of good repute, full of the Spirit and wisdom." The chosen ones were then set before the apostles, and "they prayed and ₁aid hands on them" (Acts 6:3, 6).

Later in Acts we read that the church at Antioch was instructed by the Holy Spirit: "Set apart for me Barnabas and Saul for the work to which I have called them. Then after fasting and praying they laid their hands on them and sent them off" (Acts 13:1, 2–3).

Still later, in the pastoral epistles of 1 and 2 Timothy, which were written after public patterns of religious leadership had become more formalized, the author writes of Timothy's ministry as a gift he received "when the council of elders laid their hands" upon him (1 Tim. 4:14). The gift "through the laying on of hands" endowed Timothy with "a spirit of power and love and self-control" (2 Tim. 1:6–7).

These texts, and the habits of Christian history, give the one who becomes ordained special gifts, burdens, and status. Protestants and Roman Catholics, Orthodox and Pentecostals, sacramental communities and free church bodies persist in ordaining their leaders. Only the Quakers (when they are true to their most radical ideals about the inner light in every person), the Mormons (who require every male to spend two years in a ministry of evangelism), and the Christian Scientists (who authorize readers and practitioners but do not ordain) have abolished the practice of ordination. Why? What is meant by ordination today and why is it increasingly difficult to justify or to abolish it?

An analogy with marriage may be helpful. In earlier history the freedom to choose a spouse was limited. One did not just fall in love and get married. Elders arranged marriages. Circumstances of economic status, education, geography, age, or physical appearance determined marriage. Most people got married for very practical, rather than romantic, reasons. They did not anguish over whether they were marrying the "right" person. Yet they regularly created good marriages within limited options. Furthermore, once they married, people stayed married for life, "till death them did part."

Today, things are different. Modern couples expect practical compatibility *and* romantic and sexual satisfaction. People guard their independence, trying to keep all their options open. Although marriage is entered with the assumption that it is a lifelong commitment, divorce is very common. Marriage today is a matter of individual choice balancing needs for personal intimacy, sexual expression, economic support, procreation, and status. And most of the time it is difficult for marriage to live up to the expectations people have of it.

Ordination has a similar problem. In earlier periods of history people were ordained as a result of circumstances as much as personal choice. Perhaps parents or grandparents were ministers. Often younger sons received encouragement to seek vocations in the church, inasmuch as the family inheritance went to the eldest son. Sometimes going into the ministry, like going into the army, provided opportunities for education, or travel, or political influence, or socioeconomic mobility. In Protestantism especially, clergy were upper class. Ministers perpetuated intellectual elites.

Recent understandings of ordination (especially within the last hundred years) focus on the importance of the "call" to ordained ministry. And discerning God's call to ministry has become an increasingly personal matter, only secondarily circumstantial. Today individuals anguish over their gifts to discover God's call. And in response ecclesiastical authorities are asked to confirm very individualistic understandings of ministry. Theological schools exist to strengthen those individuals who believe that the Holy Spirit has marked them for ordained ministry. Seminary degrees reassure the church that candidates for ordination are adequately prepared. Although ordination is supposedly permanent, there is a great deal of ambiguity about the status of persons who cease (for some reason or other) functioning as clergy. Today, long-standing assumptions about ordination, like assumptions about marriage, are being questioned.

The History of Ordination

As a backdrop for looking at the ministry of women in the churches, it is useful to consider ways in which the practice of ordination developed in church history. Relying upon the work of Edward Schillebeeckx, I want to lift up six developments or tensions in the history of ordination.

First, scholars of the early Christian church assert that the formalizing of orders initially grew out of attempts to accommodate the Christian movement to existing Jewish practices *and* to incorporate the household social structures of the Hellenistic world. There was also a need to regulate the expanding church in each local setting, especially as the original prophets, apostles, or founders died. Early Christians built on the existing customs of both the Jewish and Gentile worlds.

In the postexilic synagogue it was common to authorize elders by having existing leaders "lay on hands" to bless the next generation of leaders. After elders were chosen, they made decisions for the community and shaped its teaching and mission. Therefore, it was quite natural for Jewish Christians to "set apart" elders to govern the community.

Whereas in the extended households of Roman Hellenistic Christians paternalistic Gentile customs were accepted and modified by the early church, Christianity cultivated a brotherhood and sisterhood of equal partners grounded in the baptism of the Holy Spirit. But early Christians also considered themselves part of the household of God in Christ Jesus, a household patterned after the patriarchal Roman household. Local leadership was always tempered by apostles, evangelists, and ambassadors from the wider church, but it followed local household mores. There was a lot of variety, because authority was not a formal matter. Everyone was called to service.[4]

By the beginning of the second century, however, leadership patterns consolidated around local *presbyteroi* (elders) and the *episkopos* (bishop). This development was not so much the institutionalizing of previously charismatic leadership as it was the transfer of wider authority to local representatives.[5]

Second, ordination became a formal means of preserving the link between the apostolic witness (those who knew Jesus firsthand) and the ongoing institutional church. As the original founders of communities died, the young churches needed to preserve the apostolic faith. Originally, apostolicity was not connected to leadership; it existed in the content of the gospel passed on, it existed in the continuity of the community in how it lived its life from generation to generation, and it existed in certain people who carried on the authority of the prophets and apostles. Ordained ministry was important, but it was only one way of keeping alive and intact the gospel of Jesus Christ. Gradually, however, after several centuries, the "apostolic succession" of ordained leaders became the primary way for the church to preserve apostolic witness.[6]

Third, ordination was a means to protect the growing Christian community from heresy. Or, if we want to put it more positively, ordination authorized the work of those who *built up* the community through preaching, admonition, and leadership. When we look at the New Testament, ordination was originally unrelated to the Eucharist or the liturgy; it emerged when the calling to share the gospel accepted by all Christians at baptism was exercised in a special way by a few. It was functional. It set apart those who promoted the faith through teaching and preaching within the church.[7]

Fourth, ordained persons had civic responsibilities. As the church became institutionalized it took on the imperial structures of its environment. With changes in civic life, the church's ministry developed from collegial rule by presbyters to a hierarchy of bishops and metropolitans, and finally, in the West, to the supreme rule of the bishop at Rome, the pope. During times of political unrest and upheaval the resulting ecclesiastical hierarchy kept more than the faith. It upheld the stability of society in the face of chaos. Scholars have noted that "this was a legitimate, though not a necessary, development in the church."[8]

Fifth, ordination became increasingly associated with the sacramental mysteries of the Eucharist. At first there was a natural link between the ordained Christian leader and the community celebrating the Eucharist. Tertullian insisted that in order to preserve the unity of the church Christians should not receive the sacrament of the Eucharist from anyone other than the president of the community. The rule was important because a "heretical community" had no right to the Eucharist. Ordained ministry always existed within the community.[9]

Gradually, however, ordained ministry took on an objective quality. A theology of ministry developed which argued that the priest received special power through the laying on of hands, and through him the mysteries of the faith found expression. Early objections to any form of "absolute consecration" (i.e., ordination unrelated to a particular community) faded. The idea that clergy entered a new "state of life" following ordination promoted an ontological distinction between laity and clergy. Ordination endowed each priest with an indelible mark. And over time a belief in "absolute ordination" led to the great distortions of Christian community in the Middle Ages. One positive benefit, however, rested in the affirmation that the sacramental authority of the priest did not depend upon his personal worthiness or perfection. God's grace was a gift undeserved by everyone, even the clergy.[10]

Finally, sixth, with the belief that ordination bestowed an objective power on priests so that they alone could celebrate the liturgy or forgive sins, the gap between priesthood and laity widened. An emphasis on the church as the community of the spirit was replaced by a view of the church as the body of Christ. And when that happened it obscured the fact that baptism, rather than the Eucharist, is the deciding event in Christian life. Baptism stands behind all ideas of ministry and ordination. Unfortunately an overemphasis on the Christological foundation for ministry eroded its source in the living reality of the community of believers, who are all called to ministry by the Spirit.[11]

There are many more things that could be said about ordination. But for the first sixteen centuries in Western Europe the Christian church debated the meaning of ministry and ordination in these six ways: (1) Ordination ordered the local leadership of the church, but at the same time it often denied the gifts of the wider church. (2) Ordination sought to preserve the apostolic witness, but as apostolicity became equated with the direct succession of bishops it narrowed definitions of apostolicity to the succession of ordained ministers. (3) Ordination did protect against heresy, but the theological insights of certain groups lost legitimacy within the church. (4) Ordination engaged the civic order, but in so doing the church perpetuated cultural patterns of hierarchy and patriarchy. (5) Ordination mediated the sacred mysteries, but by setting apart priests to an *absolute* ordination it eventually removed ordained ministry from its communal context. (6) Finally, ordination recognized the fact that priesthood calls clergy to model a better life, but it also exacerbated artificial divisions between clergy and laity.

By the sixteenth century there were great distortions and problems with the church and its ministry in Western Europe. The control of the Roman hierarchy had confined the faith to the institutional church. Protestant Reformers, especially Luther and Calvin, challenged that power and tradition. For Luther only two things mattered: the Bible and the faith. Faith in Christ depends upon the Bible, not on the church and its clergy; and every Christian is called to ministry—that is, to share the faith. Luther argued that all Christian believers are ministers, servants, priests, by virtue of their faith in the Word of God, but every believer cannot assume the function of preaching, teaching, and counseling. Therefore, for the sake of order, certain ones must be set apart by the community of faith to undertake the office of preacher.[12]

Officially the sixteenth-century Reformers rejected patterns of hierarchical priesthood and all substantive distinctions between the clergy and the laity. Although preachers held an office that set them apart from their fellow Christians, they did so only in order to perform a duty that any Christian was entitled to fulfill. At the same time, however, the ministerial office was always rendered in the name of God and not in the name of humanity. Once appointed to the office, a minister could not be removed from it, even by the congregation that had called him, except if he disregarded or defied the Word of God. Luther insisted that every Christian has the power to forgive sins, but no one should exercise this power unless publicly authorized to do so. All the Reformers promoted a high concept of the ministry, yet they also assumed that the Christian community had great power *over* the ministry.[13]

As the sixteenth century unfolded there were many ways in which these ideas about ministry took concrete form. Probably the most influential pattern emerged in Geneva, where John Calvin argued that there was biblical warrant for four church offices: preachers, teachers, elders, and deacons. All these offices were responsible to the congregation and to God. The preachers (or pastors) were to preach, teach, and administer the sacraments. Along with the elders, they also served on the consistory, which had the responsibility to administer church discipline. The teachers were officers of the church in charge of the Academy, where young men prepared for the ministry. And finally, the deacons administered poor relief and benevolences. This fourfold pattern of orders was considered divinely prescribed and became a model for Protestant churches in France, Holland, Hungary, and Scotland. Later it was embraced by the English Puritans and adapted to the American church. It stands behind much Presbyterian practice to this day.[14]

The nature and source of the power or authority of all ministry were bestowed by the congregation. Ordination was not a sacrament, and it did not convey any absolute status. In principle, the congregational call of a minister was more important than ordination, which only confirmed the call and election. The "laying on of hands" was understood as a gesture of intercession on behalf of the ministry. Calvin wrote that "the significance of the imposition of hands is to admonish the person ordained that he is no longer his own master but devoted to the service of God and the Church." This was because Calvin regarded the power and authority of the minister as divine. An ordained minister did not speak or act in his own name; he acted in the name of God.[15]

From the sixteenth century to the early twentieth century, Protestants, especially those within the Reformed community, have sustained a creative tension between objective and functional definitions of ministry. Reformed Protestant preachers in the English-speaking world were called "ministers," ceasing to belong to the caste of "Anglican" or Roman Catholic clergy.[16] Furthermore, they were identified with the rising middle-class city merchants. Very few of the nobility became Protestant preachers. Instead, ordained ministers came from the families of teachers, clerks, printers, and weavers. Protestant ministers were encouraged to marry, and "the family life of the ministers became the symbolic expression of the communal character of the evangelical faith." Finally, the new symbol of the Protestant Christian minister was his manner of dress, the gown of the secular scholar commonly worn by men of learning among the burghers.[17]

The Ordination of Women

As we can see, tensions and ambiguities surrounding ordination have been in the Christian church for centuries. In the last hundred and fifty years, however, women have further complicated the situation. Christian women have come to the conclusion that they have a personal calling *to* and a talent *for* ordained ministry. Although many ecclesiastical authorities and traditions have not agreed that women can or should serve as ordained ministers or priests, more and more women have sought ordination. The desire of women to be ordained has aggravated longstanding tensions around ordination.

The statistics are well known, but let us review what has happened. In 1853 a small Congregational church in South Butler, New York, ordained Antoinette Brown to the Christian ministry. This is generally recognized as the first ordination of a woman in a major Christian ecclesiastical tradition. Other American women in Unitarian, Universalist, Northern Baptist, and Disciples churches sought and gained ordination in the latter half of the nineteenth century. However, at the beginning of the twentieth century less than one half of one percent of all clergy in America were women. Most of these women were outside the Reformed tradition, serving Pentecostal, holiness, or paramilitary groups like the Salvation Army. After a long and complex struggle, in the 1950s the Methodists and several Presbyterian groups voted to ordain women to ministries of Word and sacrament. It took another fifteen to twenty years before major Lutheran denominations and the Episcopalians approved the ordination of women. Roman Catholic women are still seeking admission to the priesthood.[18]

Presbyterian debates around ordination are especially complicated because of the pattern of fourfold ministry that had been handed down from Calvin. Over the years the role of preacher and teacher ceased to be differentiated, and Presbyterian churches simply ordained "teaching elders" to one ministry of Word and sacrament. Yet Presbyterians and other Reformed churches continued to ordain laypersons as deacons and ruling elders. This practice created two kinds of ordination: ordination to lay responsibilities and ordination to "clergy" status and function. In Presbyterian bodies, therefore, the struggle for the ordination of women took place at several levels.

The issue first surfaced around the question of women speaking in mixed meetings, or what were called "promiscuous assemblies." With the enthusiasm of nineteenth-century frontier revivalism, traditional understandings of women's role changed. Women's work in voluntary benevolent, humanitarian, and missionary societies generated rising controversy about women's proper participation in the church. In 1832 a "pastoral letter" concerning the dangers of revivalism was sent by the General Assembly to the churches. It contained three sentences about women:

> Meetings of pious women by themselves, for conversation and prayer, whenever they can conveniently be held, we entirely approve. But let not the inspired prohibitions of the great apostle to the Gentiles, as found in his epistles to the Corinthians and to Timothy, be violated. To teach and exhort, or to lead in prayer, in public and promiscuous assemblies, is clearly forbidden to women in the Holy Oracles.[19]

Yet everyone did not agree with this judgment, and the work of women increasingly suggested that women deserved more public roles in the churches. By the 1870s controversies developed around inviting female Quaker preachers and temperance workers to speak before many northern Presbyterian congregations. In the 1880s the newest biblical scholarship addressed the question, and many scholars concluded that there were no biblical reasons to limit women's ministries.[20]

Conservative Presbyterianism, however, was slow to respond. Although some denominations (Lutherans and

German Reformed churches) recognized that there was biblical warrant for a female deaconate and established special deaconess orders for women in health care, social work, and urban parish service by the end of the nineteenth century, Presbyterians were reluctant. In 1890 the northern Presbyterian Church in the U.S.A. proposed an overture which affirmed the apostolic origins of deaconesses and specified that they should be "elected," not ordained. It was defeated. Presbyterians were suspicious, as one writer put it, of "the odor of a Catholic nunnery which might surround an order of Protestant deaconesses." Yet over the next thirty years most of the various Presbyterian denominations modified their constitutions to provide for female deacons: the United Presbyterian Church of North America in 1906, the Cumberland Presbyterian Church in 1921, and the Presbyterian Church in the U.S.A. in 1923.[21]

Middle-class Presbyterian women, however, did not flock to become deaconesses. In keeping with Reformed concern about education, Presbyterians founded schools for education and by the early twentieth century encouraged women to prepare for an emerging lay professional position known as "Director of Christian Education" (D.C.E.). By 1938 the General Assembly of the Presbyterian Church in the U.S.A. established a category of "commissioned church worker" to recognize the Director of Religious Education (D.R.E.). It was clearly stated, however, that this status did not "confer any ministerial rights and privileges." Commissioning was different from ordination.[22]

With "ruling elders" the situation was more ambiguous. All Presbyterian bodies continued to "ordain" lay leadership to a ministry of governance. This practice was grounded in the sixteenth-century principle of the "priesthood of all believers," which ran deep within Presbyterian life. It was also supported by American democratic ideals. Furthermore, "ordination" as a "ruling elder" was permanent; even when lay leaders ceased to hold elected office as part of the session, they continued to serve local congregations in special ways because of their ordination.

The populist Cumberland Presbyterian Church struggled with the question of female ruling elders in the last
decade of the nineteenth century. Several local churches
elected women to their sessions, but these women were
repeatedly denied status as commissioners at synods and
General Assemblies. At about the same time, a woman
named Louisa Woosley convinced the Nolin (Kentucky)
Presbytery of the Cumberland Presbyterian Church that
she had a call to serve as more than a "ruling elder." In
November 1889, Louisa Woosley became the first Presbyterian woman of record to be ordained to the full work of
the gospel ministry by any presbytery. Yet the church continued to argue about the validity of her ordination. Not
until 1921 was the issue finally put to rest with a decision
that the word *man,* in scripture and in the Constitution of
the church, includes all human beings, "whether male or
female."[23] Because of Presbyterian polity, the question of
ordaining female "ruling elders" invariably became linked
to the ordination of women as "teaching elders," or ministers of Word and sacrament.

The final chapters of the story focus on the 1920s, 1950s,
and 1960s. In the '20s the Presbyterian Church in the
U.S.A. reorganized and consolidated its mission work by
absorbing the independent women's mission boards into
the general bureaucracy of the church. Many women, and
concerned men, questioned the decision and the process
leading to such a unilateral takeover. There was growing
support for changes in government that would give women
more equality. In 1926 the General Council commissioned
a study that eventually produced a report entitled *Causes
of Unrest Among Women of the Church.* Written by two
highly respected lay women, the report acknowledged that
although there was no comprehensive, organized, or articulate movement for change in the church, northern Presbyterian women wanted the "artificial inhibitions that
savor of another century" removed, so that they might be
free to "take their place wherever and however their abili-
ties and the need of the church" might call.

The report led to a conference and finally to a series of

overtures from the General Assembly that were sent to the presbyteries for vote. In brief, there were three overtures, three choices: (A) full equality for women as ordained ruling elders and as ministers of Word and sacrament; (B) approval of women as ruling elders but not as teaching elders; and (C) the approval of women as licensed evangelists. In the end only Overture B was approved, giving women full lay status but denying them ordination to the ministry of Word and sacrament. Observers have noted that the action was neither reactionary or radical. In the name of conservatism Overture A was defeated, while in the name of progressivism Overture B was approved.[24] Women could be "ordained," but they could not be *really* ordained.

In 1947 the question of women's ordination came back to the General Assembly. At that time, however, postwar idealism about women's place in the home created an unreceptive environment. The overture was defeated. Finally, in 1955 as the need for more clergy grew during the religious revival of the 1950s, an overture to ordain women as "teaching elders" (clergy) was proposed *and* ratified by an overwhelming majority.

Although it was a victory, many of those who voted for women ministers doubted that great numbers of women would ever seek ordination. Women, they thought, were destined to serve in education, in rural settings, in the urban crisis, and as assistants to established clergy. Rather than being a vote for the equality of women in ministry, it was viewed as a vote driven by expediency.

Over the next decade Presbyterian church mergers and the dream of reunion between the largest northern and southern Presbyterian denominations pushed the approval of women's ordination along. When the Presbyterian Church in the U.S.A. merged with the smaller United Presbyterian Church in North America in 1958, women were granted full ordination as ruling and teaching elders. This happened in spite of the fact that United Presbyterians had never done either.[25] In the (southern) Presbyterian Church in the U.S., although women had served on national committees and boards, in its entire history the southern Presbyterian Church had never even ordained women as deacons. It was understandable, however, that in 1957, shortly after the northern church had approved full ordination for women, a measure was sent to the southern presbyteries asking for approval of the ordination of women as deacons and ruling elders. Predictably, the more conservative southern church voted it down. Finally, in 1964 the Presbyterian Church in the U.S. approved the ordination of women as deacons, ruling elders, and ministers all at once. As in the northern church, however, few southern Presbyterians expected that many women would seek ordination in order to become pastors.[26] It was hoped, however, that the issue of women's ordination would not be a barrier to the long-awaited reunion of northern and southern Presbyterian churches. Today the newly organized Presbyterian Church (U.S.A.) supports the ordination of women to all orders.

Since the early 1970s the enrollment of women in theological seminaries has dramatically increased—women were under 5 percent in 1972 preordination programs; they were 22 percent in 1988. The shift is even more dramatic when we compare the number of male and female seminary graduates earning the Master of Divinity degree during the last decade. In 1977, 462 women graduated (8.4 percent), whereas in 1987, 1,496 women graduated (21.4 percent). This increase in the number of female M.Div. graduates (224 percent) contrasts sharply with the fact that during the same period of time the number of male seminary graduates increased very little (4.6 percent). In 1987, 33.5 percent of all Presbyterian seminary graduates were women. This percentage reflects a pattern shared by many mainline Protestant denominations: Women were 38.1 percent of United Methodist graduates, 30.4 percent of Disciples, 29.8 percent of American Baptists, 36.4 percent of Episcopalians, and 47.6 percent of United Church of Christ graduates. Not all women who graduate from seminary seek ordination, but many of them do.[27]

Ordination from the Woman's Perspective

In my research on women and ordination I have been examining the efforts of women to gain ordination in mainline Protestant denominations like the Presbyterians, but I have also sought to understand the experience of ordination from women's perspective. How do women appropriate the meaning of ordination and make it their own?

Let me speak autobiographically to set the stage. I grew up in a Congregational church in the 1950s. Active in the youth program of that large church in Detroit, Michigan, during high school, I decided that I was going to be a minister. I loved the church and, to be honest, I also loved (or had a teenage crush on) the young associate minister. I had never seen a woman minister, but I wanted to be one. I wanted to continue the sense of excitement, meaning, and community that I found in my church. I was not out to prove anything. I certainly was not a feminist. I was simply a young girl with a desire to share my experience of God and church with others. There was no dramatic call or decisive moment. I found myself naturally growing toward a vocational role in church service.

To make a long story short, during my senior year in high school I "went in care" as a candidate for the "Christian ministry"; and seven years later, after four years of college and three years of seminary, I returned to Mayflower Congregational Church to be ordained. That was twenty-five years ago, in 1964. What did I think I was doing? I realize now that I was not very self-conscious about ordination. It was a ritual and a status that celebrated *my* love affair with the church, but I did not bother a great deal about its historical, theological, or ecumenical meaning. By that time I was married to a man who planned to be a college professor and so I pragmatically decided that I would be a campus minister.

As the 1960s flowed into the 1970s the question of women's ordination became more visible and I became more reflective. I watched the difficulties surrounding ordination for Episcopal women. I read a great deal in the literature of the women's liberation movement. I began to see how women were challenging some of the unexamined assumptions about ordination. I began to meet women who had struggled against prejudice and hostility to become ordained, only to find that it was an ambiguous victory. Ordination carries so many patriarchal assumptions that women find themselves increasingly ambivalent about its value. As one woman put it, "When I was not ordained I thought I needed its recognition and authority, but now that I've got it, I question any ecclesiology or theology of ministry that needs it." For many women today the vocational crisis is not whether the church will ordain them but whether they *want* to be ordained. The critique women bring to ordination relates to many of the issues embedded in my earlier discussion of the history of ordination. Three areas of tension are worth exploring more specifically.

First, there has been an ongoing tension between ordination as local and ordination as universal. In the earliest eras of church history, ordination (the specific setting apart of some persons by prayer and laying on of hands) was to empower local leaders *and* to enable evangelistic witness beyond the local setting. Initially, local clergy were connected to the community, and the people insisted that eucharistic acts should not be conducted without clergy present; later, the argument was reversed and the Eucharist became invalid unless ordained leaders presided.

Women today are questioning all objective and universal definitions of ordination. They have noted the self-contradiction and incoherence of theologies of priesthood and ministry that "twist the humility of Christ into a religion of power."[28] They have come to the conclusion that the issue is not whether women can become priests or bishops; the issue is the "transformation of our religious institutions." How can women (and men) "convert Christianity to the gender-free faith which they are certain Jesus intended?" *Newsweek* magazine has noted that putting women in the pulpit is no longer the prime goal of Christian feminists. Rather, the aim is a "thorough comprehensive transformation of the language, symbols, and sacred texts of the Christian faith."[29] Ordination is seriously questioned because, as one Episcopal radical feminist writes, "ordination *in itself* does not bestow the least spiritual authority, personal holiness, specialized knowledge of ways into God, or privileged access to God. Neither does ordination bestow prerogatives of coercive power."[30]

Women clergy in particular find that the "set apart" traditions of ordination perpetuate patterns of hierarchy that are increasingly dysfunctional in mainline white churches. Women choose to reject ontological definitions of "absolute consecration," and women also are moving beyond viewing ordination as merely personal choice or local service.

The work of contemporary scholars in the psychology field suggests some new ways to think about ordination that transcend both ontological and functional perspectives. Jean Baker Miller, author of *Toward a New Psychology of Women,* notes that women are seeking autonomy, but they want something more complete than "autonomy as men have defined it." Women want deeper relationships and holistic selfhood at the same time. It seems to me that many of the recent insights from the new psychology of women found in the writings of Mary Field Belenky, Blythe McVicker Clinchy, Nancy Rule Goldberger, Jill Mattuck Tarule, Nancy Chodorow, and Carol Gilligan describe how women may be appropriating and transforming historic definitions of ordination.[31]

If women thrive on relationships and the fullness of life comes when they can weave themselves into a web of strong relationships that are empowering, activating, honest, and close, then ordained women will define the function and the status of ordained ministry differently. This is consistent with recent work in women's psychology that describes patterns of "mutual empathy" or "intersubjectivity."

Standard developmental psychology (as well as predominant understandings of calling to ordination) tends to stress development as a process of individuation, independence, and autonomy. These characteristics are the marks of psychological maturity (and of spiritual discernment). Yet when women are measured by such standards they are considered relatively immature and dependent. Carol Gilligan's book *In a Different Voice* and Mary Belenky's (and others') study of epistemology in *Women's Ways of Knowing* argue that men make moral decisions by thinking about rights while most women make moral choices by thinking and feeling about webs of responsibilities within relationships.[32]

For women, "relationality" is basic, yet the entire culture devalues relationships while expecting women to specialize in them. We should not be surprised, therefore, that ordination for women produces the same double bind. To be set apart by prayer and laying on of hands is an isolating communal act. Women need to keep relationality and enlarge the relational context, rather than focus upon separation and exclusivity.[33]

Lynn Rhodes, interviewing clergywomen for her book *Co-Creating: A Feminist Vision of Ministry,* found that clergywomen did not tie their sense of vocation to being ordained. In the context of community, clergywomen know that ordination does influence the way they are perceived and they cherish the gifts they receive because they are ordained. However, Rhodes writes, for them the issue is not to deny the value of such relationships, or the power they have, but to extend the possibility that other people of the community can also be seen as trustworthy and as having resources and strength for one another in times of crisis. In that sense, the clergyperson is not any more a "representative" than anyone else who identifies with the community. The issue, as one woman put it, is how "we *all* model with and for each other the meaning of our lives."[34]

A United Church of Christ pastor shared with me her vision of ordained ministry as leadership for the upbuilding of the faithful *community.* It is not just being pastoral to individuals. The ordained one is literally called to "cure the soul of the church," to provide vision, to show the way during a time of declining expectations.

Like many women clergy, this pastor is especially concerned about the marginalization of the laity. Unfortunately, she notes, local and wider church life is all structured to pull people in and to build up the institutional church. This is backwards. The church is the body Christ gathered for worship *and* scattered over the face of the earth as disciples and ministers of Jesus Christ. All are baptized to an outreach ministry, and the ordained clergy exist to "equip the saints for the work of ministry" (Eph. 4:13–16).

This pastor insists, therefore, that the ordained are not the "set apart" ones. At baptism every Christian has been set apart. Whereas at ordination some are set "in the midst of" those who are set apart—set in the midst to serve and equip the church for ministry. She concludes, "As a Christian I do participate in the 'power of the sacred,' but no more so than any other person who is self-consciously 'in Christ.' "[35]

From the earliest decades of the church, the tensions between the local and wider church, between personal salvation and institutional nurture, between individual integrity and relational needs, and between laity and clergy have shaped understandings of ordination. Women bring significant insights to these concerns in our times.

Second, there has been an ongoing tension over whether ordination has more to do with ministries of the Word or ministries at the sacramental table. In the earliest era, almost all scholars agree, acts of "ordination" had nothing to do with sacraments; ordination authorized preaching and teaching. Over the centuries, however, ordination has increasingly been connected with sacramental leadership. Although the general Protestant insistence that ordination is not a sacrament and the Reformed traditions around the ordination of ruling elders have tempered this trend, ecumenical developments have emphasized that ordination is to priestly leadership at the Eucharist, or Lord's Supper.

This is very interesting. In the development of American Protestantism there has been a great deal of latitude about the relationship of ordination to preaching. Schoolteachers and other learned leaders in the Reformed tradition preached in many colonial pulpits, but they refused to preside over the Lord's Supper. Why? Given our Reformed theology it ought to be the other way around. Methodism licensed local preachers but only allowed ordained elders to administer the sacrament without restrictions. Early on, women evangelists and lecturers were allowed to preach and teach, but when they sought ordination there was a problem. Why?

In the modern post-Enlightenment era some of the ambiguity about ordination relates to our understanding of professions and recent efforts to define ministry as a profession.

William F. May, of Southern Methodist University, suggests that there are tensions between a Christian vocation, a profession, and a career. Every Christian has a vocation, which as traditionally conceived involves a commitment to God and neighbor. A career, however, is a more selfish thing; it is a means to pursue one's own private aims and purposes. Instead of asking what is the need of the community, a career orientation asks what do *I* want to be? Where do *I* want to go?[36]

The professional, and we like to think of ministry as a profession, stands somewhere between the vocation and the career. Originally the word "profess" meant literally "to testify on behalf of," or "to stand for something." For this reason being a "professional" carries implications about knowledge and moral responsibility. The professional knows something that will benefit the wider community, and he or she has a responsibility to use that knowledge to serve the wider human community. Yet professional services always involve an uneven interaction between the professional and the client. For this reason, as May puts it, a healthy professional exchange requires that the professional be "sufficiently distanced from his/her own interests and convenience to serve the client's own well-being."[37]

Good professionals also know more than others about some things. There is an elitism built into all professional work. Professionals have information that average ordinary people do not have. And they develop what May calls "cognitive superiority which spills over into a form of moral disdain for the client." In response the professional relationship cultivates a passivity in those who are not "in the know."[38]

It is not surprising, therefore, that for many women a heavy emphasis on the ordained ministry as a "profession" creates a problem. Women, who have often been clients, or even victims, in professional relationships are especially sensitive to the uneven power dynamics of ordination in the church. If the emphasis is on the ministry of the Word, there are dangers of intellectual elitism that keep laity passive and clergy in control. If the emphasis is on a more sacramental ministry, there are dangers of institutional isolation from ministry in the world.

One way out of the elitism implicit in ordination to ministries of the Word is to recapture the importance of teaching as well as preaching. Preaching seeks transformation. But transformational leadership in all professions runs the danger of paternalism. As May notes, "The professional who insists on transforming the client's behavior, but who neglects to *teach* the client inevitably relies on managerial, manipulative and condescending modes of behavior control."[39] This is something women know all too well.

When ministry focuses on teaching, rather than preaching, however, the professional relationship is different. The act of teaching engages the other with respect. It treats the other as a whole human self and builds up the church for service in the world. Teaching, not preaching, should stand at the core of authentic ministry.

Another way out of the isolation and irresponsibility sometimes found in ordination to sacramental ministries is to shift the sacramental focus. Protestantism upholds two biblically based sacraments—baptism and the Eucharist (or Lord's Supper or Communion). Most discussions about ordination and the sacraments revolve around the Table—not around baptism.

But what would happen if the sacramental center of the church and its major ecclesiastical energy was focused on baptism rather than Communion? Women have suggested that some of their difficulty with ordained sacramental leadership would be changed by such an emphasis. We are all called to ministry through our baptism. There is neither lay nor ordained, there is neither male nor female, all are equal in the Spirit through baptism.

If ministry of the Word was viewed as a ministry of teaching *and* preaching, and if the ministry of sacraments focused on baptism rather than the Table, ordination would carry a very different meaning. Theologically we say that laity and ordained persons are called to exercise differing forms of the one ministry of Christ which is shared by the whole people of God. Recent ecumenical theology begins with this basic truth but continues to insist on the historic orders of bishop, presbyter, and deacon. Traditions around those orders for women are not helpful.

It is not surprising, therefore, that ordained women are very wary that a theology of ministry grounded in the priesthood of all believers will still be subverted. As the *COCU Consensus* puts it, "Lay status in the Church is not a residual status, but rather the primary form of ministry apart from which no other Christian ministry can be described." Laity must never be defined as the ones who are "not ordained" or "not professional." Clergy and laity have Christian vocations each with special responsibilities.[40]

From the earliest decades of the church the tensions between Word and sacrament, between teaching and preaching, between baptism and the Lord's Supper, between laity and clergy have shaped understandings of ordination. Women bring significant insights into these concerns in our times.

Finally, there has been an ongoing tension around the relationship between the office and the person of the ordained minister. This is because the ordination of women calls for renewed recognition of the power of sexuality in human community, especially in the church. In a Professional Ethics research group which I am part of in Berkeley, California, we have surveyed male and female clergy on questions of sexual ethics and issues of homosexuality, ordination, and ministry.

Women, especially clergywomen, insist that an ethic of sexual behavior cannot be divorced from issues of power and from affirmations of sexuality as part of God's good creation. Yet in Western society, women have always been associated with the "lower" or "lesser" forces that perpetuate the struggles between culture and nature, or between spirit and flesh. As such, women often see power from the underside, and therefore women clergy feel that they are able to relate to powerlessness more effectively.

Simply being an ordained woman challenges the cultural habit of separating sexuality and spirituality. Because she is a woman in a culture that does not value women, an ordained woman must come to terms with her sexuality in ways that male clergy can avoid. Women clergy must affirm the goodness of sexuality in the process of affirming themselves.

Ordained women ministers also remind us of the connection between sexuality and power. As ordained persons they hold the power of position; as women they find their power denied or usurped. When we asked ordained women about sexual ethical dilemmas in their work, we found that women are much more concerned with defending themselves than they are worried about the power or danger of their own sexual improprieties. The larger culture assumes that women will set the boundaries in sexual encounters, and clergywomen continue to carry that responsibility.[41]

In traditional understandings of ordination the character and personal ethics of clergy are expected to be exemplary. This is true for men and women. Women clergy, however, are finding important connections between eros, power, and spirituality. Rita Nakashima Brock writes in her new book *Journeys by Heart: A Christology of Erotic Power*[42] that the erotic power women experience through their own feelings and bodies *is* in many cases a relationship with God. Women are restoring the trustworthiness of eros, a life/love force known to them through their relationships with one another. Women refuse to suppress sexuality as a dangerous evil force and find that it is the foundation of the relationality they value.

From the earliest decades of the church, tensions between body and spirit, between the carnal and the holy, and between power and weakness have shaped understandings of ordination. Women bring significant insights into these concerns in our times.

The Reformed tradition has made strong contributions to the theology and practice of ministry since the sixteenth century. In its willingness to retrieve the importance of the priesthood of all believers, and in its decisions to ordain women to ministries of Word and sacrament, it has challenged and will continue to enrich our understanding of some of the long-standing tensions around the practice of ordination.

Women in ministry:

Question all universal, indelible, power-focused understandings of ordination

Identify with theories of women's psychology that uphold autonomy without sacrificing relationality

Seek to extend ministry beyond institutional maintenance

View themselves as "set in the midst" of the faithful community rather than "set apart"

Are wary of professional definitions of ministry that rely on patterns of elitism and dependency

Affirm the importance of teaching, which transforms without patronizing

Celebrate the sacrament of baptism, which ordains all Christians to ministry

Reject understandings of laity as "non-clergy" or "non-professional"

Refuse to separate sexuality, spirituality, and power

Recognize that character and ethical standards are part of Christian discipleship

Many men do these same things, but I am convinced that as more and more women attend seminary and confront the question of ordination, our definitions and practices related to ordination will change. It is not yet clear exactly what will happen, but something is happening.

Notes

Series Foreword

1. Arthur M. Schlesinger, Sr., "A Critical Period in American Religion, 1875–1900," first appeared in the *Massachusetts Historical Society Proceedings* 64 (1930–32) and is reprinted in John M. Mulder and John F. Wilson, eds., *Religion in American History: Interpretive Essays* (Englewood Cliffs, N.J.: Prentice-Hall, 1978), pp. 302–317.

2. Robert T. Handy, "The American Religious Depression, 1925–1935," *Church History* 29 (1960), 3–16, reprinted in Mulder and Wilson, *Religion in American History*, pp. 431–444; Handy, *A Christian America: Protestant Hopes and Historical Realities*, 2nd ed. (New York: Oxford University Press, 1984), pp. 159–184.

3. Sydney E. Ahlstrom, "The Radical Turn in Theology and Ethics: Why It Occurred in the 1960s," *Annals of the American Academy of Political and Social Science* 387 (1970), 1–13, reprinted in Mulder and Wilson, *Religion in American History*, pp. 445–456; Ahlstrom, "The Traumatic Years: American Religion and Culture in the 1960s and 1970s," *Theology Today* 26 (1980), 504–522; Ahlstrom, *A Religious History of the American People* (New Haven: Yale University Press, 1972), pp. 1079–1096.

4. Wade Clark Roof and William McKinney, *American Mainline Religion: Its Changing Shape and Future* (New Brunswick, N.J.: Rutgers University Press, 1987); Robert Wuthnow, *The Re-*

structuring of American Religion: Society and Faith Since World War II (Princeton, N.J.: Princeton University Press, 1988).

5. John V. Taylor, *The Primal Vision: Christian Presence Amid African Religion* (Philadelphia: Fortress Press, 1964), chapter 13, "The Practice of Presence " pp. 196–205.

Introduction

1. Wade Clark Roof and William McKinney, *American Mainline Religion: Its Changing Shape and Future* (New Brunswick, N.J.: Rutgers University Press, 1987); and Robert Wuthnow, *The Restructuring of American Religion: Society and Faith Since World War II* (Princeton, N.J.: Princeton University Press, 1988); see also William R. Hutchison, ed., *Between the Times: The Travail of the Protestant Establishment in America, 1900–1960* (Cambridge: Cambridge University Press, 1989).

1: The Restructuring of American Presbyterianism

1. Robert Wuthnow, *The Restructuring of American Religion: Society and Faith Since World War II* (Princeton, N.J.: Princeton University Press, 1988).

2. I have drawn this summary primarily from Sydney E. Ahlstrom, *A Religious History of the American People* (New Haven, Conn.: Yale University Press, 1972), pp. 267–279, 462–471.

3. These conclusions are from Robert C. Liebman, John R. Sutton, and Robert Wuthnow, "Exploring the Social Sources of Denominationalism: Schisms in American Protestant Denominations, 1890–1980," *American Sociological Review* 53 (1988), 343–352. Some additional findings are given in John R. Sutton, Robert Wuthnow, and Robert C. Liebman, "Organizational Foundings: Schisms in American Protestant Denominations, 1890–1980," presented at the 1988 meetings of the American Sociological Association in Atlanta, Georgia. Copies of these and subsequent papers can be obtained from John R. Sutton, Department of Sociology, University of California, Santa Barbara, California.

4. These data were calculated from the 1960 and 1976 National Election Surveys. The National Election Surveys are conducted by the Center for Political Studies at the University of Michigan. Major surveys are conducted every four years during Presidential elections; minor surveys are conducted midway between the ma-

jor studies during Congressional elections. The data analyzed were on tapes at the Princeton University Computer Center. These tapes are available through the Inter-University Consortium for Political and Social Research at the University of Michigan. On the other hand, mean family incomes for Presbyterians were 1.14 times the national average in 1960, and 1.35 in 1980.

5. The 1956 data are from the national survey conducted by the Census Bureau in that year, as reported in Bernard Lazerwitz, "Religion and Social Structure in the United States," in *Religion, Culture and Society: A Reader in the Sociology of Religion,* ed. Louis Schneider (New York: John Wiley & Sons, 1964), pp. 426–439. The 1980 figures were derived from the National Election Survey data from that year.

6. From the author's analysis of the General Social Survey Cumulative Data File for the years 1972–1982.

7. These data are also from an analysis of the General Social Survey Cumulative Data File, 1972–1982. They are based on nearly 12,000 cases from representative adult samples of the U.S. population.

8. The data for the 1950s are reported in Andrew M. Greeley, *The Denominational Society* (Glenview, Ill.: Scott, Foresman & Co., 1972), p. 245. The data for the 1970s are from an analysis of the General Social Survey Cumulative File, 1972–1982.

9. Ware W. Wimberly, "The Mixed Marriage," *Presbyterian Tribune* (January 1946), pp. 9–10.

10. I have discussed these results, which come from my analysis of nationally representative data collected in 1984 by the Gallup organization, in my book *The Restructuring of American Religion,* see especially pp. 215–225.

11. Dean R. Hoge, *Division in the Protestant House* (Philadelphia: Westminster Press, 1976).

12. *Presbyterian Layman* (July-August 1988), pp. 1, 4.

13. *Presbyterian Panel* (March 1987), p. A9.

14. *Presbyterian Panel* (September 1986), p. A3.

15. *Presbyterian Panel* (September 1987), A9.

16. Based on an analysis of 383 Presbyterians polled in General Social Surveys between 1972 and 1982.

17. Data on this question were available from 250 Presbyterians polled in the General Social Survey between 1972 and 1984.

18. *Presbyterian Layman* (July–August 1988), p. 2.

19. These results are from the 1984 national survey conducted by the Gallup organization.

20. R. Stephen Warner, *New Wine in Old Wineskins: Evangelicals and Liberals in a Small-Town Church* (Berkeley, Calif.: University of California Press, 1988).

21. Study conducted by the Research Unit of the Support Agency of the Presbyterian Church (U.S.A.), a brief report of which was published in *The Presbyterian Layman* (November–December 1987), p. 1.

22. In recent studies, elders have given conservative responses in higher proportions than pastors and other lay members on issues such as supporting the contras in Nicaragua and opposing a bilateral nuclear arms moratorium between the United States and the Soviet Union, and yet have shown no tendency toward greater conservatism on issues such as pornography and gender discrimination. See, for example, responses to the various questions reported in the *Presbyterian Panel* (March and September 1987).

23. *Presbyterian Panel* (September 1986), pp. A3, A4.

24. These results are from my analysis of General Social Survey Data collected between 1972 and 1984; the percentages are based on 117 Presbyterian women with at least some college education and 162 Presbyterian women with no college education; among Presbyterian men, no statistically significant difference in church attendance is present between those with or without college educations.

25. Specifically, 30 percent of the women who scored high on a scale of feminist attitudes said they attended church nearly every week or more often, compared with 31 percent of the women who scored low on the scale.

26. These results are from my analysis of General Social Survey data collected between 1972 and 1984; they are based on more than 700 cases of former Baptists, 800 cases of former Methodists, and 500 cases of former members of Protestant sects.

2: The Presbyterian Heritage as Modernism

1. See William E. McKinney and Wade C. Roof, "Liberal Protestantism: A Sociodemographic Perspective," in Robert S. Michaelsen and Wade Clark Roof, eds., *Liberal Protestantism: Realities and Possibilities* (New York: Pilgrim Press, 1986).

2. Martin Marty, *A Nation of Behavers* (Chicago: University of Chicago Press, 1976).

3. The notion of a shift assumes some sort of previous establishment, in this case, the hegemony of a "Protestant establishment" from colonial times into the twentieth century. For an account of the forming of this establishment, see Martin E. Marty, *Righteous Empire* (New York: Dial Press, 1970); H. Richard Niebuhr, *The Kingdom of God in America* (1937; repr. Middletown, Conn.: Wesleyan University Press, 1988); and Digby Baltzell, *The Protestant Establishment: Aristocracy and Caste in America* (New Haven, Conn.: Yale University Press, 1964; repr. 1987).

4. Much of this story is told in Martin Marty's *The New Shape of American Religion* (Westport, Conn.: Greenwood Press, 1978). But see also Robert Bellah, *Beyond Belief* (Grand Rapids: Wm. B. Eerdmans Publishing Co., 1981); and Richard D. Brown, *Modernization: The Transformation of American Life, 1600–1865* (New York: Hill & Wang, 1976).

5. The last twenty years have seen a number of works that describe the removal of the Protestant mainline to the margins of religious and cultural influence and the rise of a new and conservative religious center. One of the earliest books that called attention to the fact was Jeffrey K. Hadden's *The Gathering Storm in the Churches* (Garden City, N.Y.: Doubleday & Co., Anchor Books, 1970). But see also Dean M. Kelley, *Why Conservative Churches Are Growing* (New York: Harper & Row, 1972; repr. Macon, Ga.: Mercer University Press, 1986). Since the early works, major studies of the changed demography of American Protestantism have gotten under way. See Wade Clark Roof and William McKinney, *American Mainline Religion: Its Changing Shape and Future* (New Brunswick, N.J.: Rutgers University Press, 1987); Carl S. Dudley, *Where Have All Our People Gone? New Choices for Old Churches* (New York: Pilgrim Press, 1979); and Dean R. Hoge and David A. Roozen, eds., *Understanding Church Growth and Decline: 1950–1978* (New York: Pilgrim Press, 1979).

6. Some observers have noted mainline responses to their own decline. John R. Fry's controversial little book is largely a description of the response as it was occurring in the 1970s: *The Trivialization of the United Presbyterian Church* (New York: Harper & Row, 1975). See also John H. Leith, *The Reformed Imperative* (Philadelphia: Westminster Press, 1988), p. 21.

7. John A. Mackay, *The Presbyterian Way of Life* (Englewood Cliffs, N.J.: Prentice-Hall, 1960), p. 50.

8. Brian Gerrish, *Tradition and the Modern World* (Chicago: University of Chicago Press, 1978), p. 7.

9. One of the best histories of modernism as a strand of North American Protestant Christianity is William R. Hutchison's *The Modernist Impulse in American Protestantism* (Cambridge, Mass.: Harvard University Press, 1976).

10. Kenneth Cauthen uses the term "modernistic liberalism" to describe this form of modernism. See his *The Impact of American Religious Liberalism* (New York: Harper & Brothers, 1962; 2nd ed., Lanham, Md.: University Press of America, 1983), chapter 2.

11. Philip Rieff has described the pervasiveness of the therapeutic worldview and of "psychological man" in *The Triumph of the Therapeutic* (New York: Harper & Row, 1966; repr. Chicago: University of Chicago Press, 1987).

12. The most detailed history of the pre-World War I Presbyterian response to modernizing influence at work in the nineteenth century remains Lefferts A. Loetscher's *Broadening Church* (Philadelphia: University of Pennsylvania Press, 1964). See especially the first nine chapters. In addition see Maurice W. Armstong, Lefferts A. Loetscher, and Charles A. Anderson, eds., *The Presbyterian Enterprise* (Philadelphia: Westminster Press, 1956).

13. For the story of the controversy surrounding David Swing, see Hutchison, *The Modernist Impulse,* chapter 2.

14. See Loetscher, *Broadening Church,* chapters 3, 4, and 6.

15. Brian Gerrish's *Tradition and the Modern World* is not specifically on the response of the Reformed tradition to the sciences. It does however offer detailed studies of a group of Reformed theologians (Friedrich Schleiermacher, John W. Nevin, John McLeod Campbell, and A. E. Biedermann) whose theologies constituted a response to the changing world of the sciences and philosophy.

16. The major history of Presbyterian ecumenism is W. Stanley Rycroft's *The Ecumenical Witness of The United Presbyterian Church in the U.S.A.* (Philadelphia: Board of Christian Education of The United Presbyterian Church in the U.S.A., 1968). But see also Mackay, *The Presbyterian Way of Life,* for a strong emphasis on ecumenism in the Presbyterian heritage.

17. "The Confession of 1967," *Book of Confessions* (New York: General Assembly of the Presbyterian Church (U.S.A.), 1983).

18. Dean Hoge (Hoge and Roozen, eds., *Understanding Church Growth and Decline,* chapter 4) warns that a decade of studies do

not support the thesis that specific policies within the liberal denominations are responsible for their decline. See also chapter 9 for a similar conclusion.

19. See Roof and McKinney, *American Mainline Religion,* chapter 5

3: Congregational Identity and Mainline Protestantism

1. Two feature stories have appeared in national news magazines (Kenneth L. Woodward, "From 'Mainline' to Sideline," *Time* 108, Dec. 22, 1986, pp. 54–56; and Richard M. Ostling, "Those Mainline Blues," May 22, 1989, pp. 94–96); a number of other stories have appeared in local publications.

2. The Committee on Theological Education of the Presbyterian Church (U.S.A.), for instance, invited historian Dorothy C. Bass and sociologists Benton Johnson and Wade Clark Roof to address a meeting of the Committee. The Committee then published the lectures (*Mainstream Protestantism in the Twentieth Century: Its Problems and Prospects*; privately printed, 1986) and distributed them widely in the church.

3. James F. Hopewell surveys this literature in *Congregation: Stories and Structures,* ed. Barbara G. Wheeler (Philadelphia: Fortress Press, 1987), pp. 19–39; an earlier bibliography, compiled by Carl S. Dudley and James F. Hopewell, appears in Carl S. Dudley, ed., *Building Effective Ministry: Theory and Practice in the Local Church* (San Francisco: Harper & Row, 1983), pp. 246–257.

4. Some of the small number of studies that focus on mainline Protestant congregations are those produced by members of the Project Team for Congregational Studies, including *Building Effective Ministry* and *Congregation,* cited above, and Jackson W. Carroll, Carl S. Dudley, and William McKinney, eds., *Handbook for Congregational Studies* (Nashville: Abingdon Press, 1986). There are a few other recent analytical volumes, such as C. Ellis Nelson, ed., *Congregations: Their Power to Form and Transform* (Atlanta: John Knox Press, 1988); and David A. Roozen, William McKinney, and Jackson W. Carroll, *Varieties of Religious Presence: Mission in Public Life* (New York: Pilgrim Press, 1984).

5. For an argument that "American corporate piety" is persistently local, see William H. Swatos, Jr., "Beyond Denominationalism? Community and Culture in American Religion," *Journal for the Scientific Study of Religion* 20/3 (1981), 217–227. Swatos

thinks that "a critical error of much contemporary thinking about denominationalism is a focus upon the trans-local or national aspects of the organization" (223).

6. Melvin D. Williams, *Community in a Black Pentecostal Church: An Anthropological Study* (Prospect Heights, Ill.: Waveland Press, Inc., 1984).

7. Nancy Tatom Ammerman, *Bible Believers: Fundamentalists in the Modern World* (New Brunswick, N.J.: Rutgers University Press, 1987).

8. James Ault, Jr., and Michael Camarini, *Born Again,* 1987, available from James Ault Films, 7570 La Jolla Boulevard, La Jolla, CA 92037. See also *Miracle in Intervale,* a film about a tiny group of Orthodox Jews in a Hispanic neighborhood in the Bronx, available from the Board of Jewish Education of Greater New York, 426 West 58th Street, New York, NY 10019.

9. Steven M. Tipton, *Getting Saved from the Sixties: Moral Meaning in Conversion and Cultural Change* (Berkeley: University of California Press, 1982). Frances Fitzgerald, in her Pulitzer-prize winning book *Cities on a Hill* (New York: Simon & Schuster, Inc., 1986), is even more broadly inclusive. Her studies of "visionary communities" that she thinks extend the Puritan aspiration to create a model community and the fervor of the nineteenth-century evangelical revivals include a retirement community in Florida, Oregon's rather sinister Rajneeshpuram, and the Castro, a homosexual district in San Francisco.

10. See note 3.

11. R. Stephen Warner, *New Wine in Old Wineskins: Evangelicals and Liberals in a Small-Town Church* (Berkeley, Calif.: University of California Press, 1988).

12. Michael H. Ducey, *Sunday Morning: Aspects of Urban Ritual* (New York: Free Press, 1977).

13. Robert Wuthnow, *The Restructuring of American Religion: Society and Faith Since World War II* (Princeton, N.J.: Princeton University Press, 1988) contains a broadly inclusive bibliography of recent works on both mainline and evangelical religion, pp. 361–368.

14. Phillip E. Hammond, for instance, has proposed a new study that will, in his words, "help in understanding the rather sizable religious change going on around us." Among his guiding questions are several of the major conundrums: Why mainline decline after decades of growth? Why orthodox, evangelical expansion despite continuing secularization? Why such regional variations in

religion? He will attack these questions, he writes, by a study that consists of a telephone survey and personal interviews, "focussing on the now-maturing post-World War II birth cohort"—the baby-boomers. "Religion and the Persistence of Identity," *Journal for the Scientific Study of Religion* 27/1 (1988), 7.

15. Warner, *New Wine in Old Wineskins,* pp. 46–47.

16. Ibid., p. 47, quoting Francesco Alberoni.

17. Ibid., p. 30.

18. Douglas A. Walrath, "Social Change and Local Churches: 1961–75," in Dean R. Hoge and David A. Roozen, eds., *Understanding Church Growth and Decline: 1950–1978* (New York: Pilgrim Press, 1979), p. 269.

19. Wuthnow, *Restructuring of American Religion,* pp. 122–123.

20. Hopewell, *Congregation,* p. 4.

21. Ibid., p. 5.

22. Ibid., pp. 119–139.

23. Ammerman, *Bible Believers,* p. 212.

24. Ducey, *Sunday Morning,* pp. 160–161.

25. Warner, *New Wine in Old Wineskins,* p. 27.

26. Ducey, *Sunday Morning,* p. 136.

27. See, for instance, Roozen, McKinney, and Carroll, *Varieties of Religious Presence,* pp. 29–31. Several writers in Dudley, ed., *Building Effective Ministry,* use the concept of an open system (see the index). See also Dean R. Hoge, "A Test of Theories of Denominational Growth and Decline," in Hoge and Roozen, pp. 179–197, who tries to measure the relative influence of "internal" and "external" factors in growth and decline.

28. Dean M. Kelley, *Why Conservative Churches Are Growing* (New York: Harper & Row, 1972; repr., Macon, Ga.: Mercer University Press, 1986).

29. See especially Wade Clark Roof and William McKinney, *American Mainline Religion: Its Changing Shape and Future* (New Brunswick, N.J.: Rutgers University Press, 1987), pp. 106–185.

30. See note 18.

4: Presbyterians and Sabbath Observance

1. See, for example, Winton U. Solberg, *Redeem the Time: The Puritan Sabbath in Early America* (Cambridge, Mass.: Harvard University Press, 1977).

2. Ernest Trice Thompson, *Presbyterians in the South,* vol. 3: *1890–1972* (Richmond, Va.: John Knox Press, 1973).

3. James H. Smylie, " 'Of Secret and Family Worship': Historical Meditations, 1875–1975," *Journal of Presbyterian History,* 58 (Summer 1980), 95–115.

4. Louis B. Weeks, "The Scriptures and Sabbath Observance in the South," *Journal of Presbyterian History* 59 (Summer 1981), 267–283.

5. I have made use of several college, university, seminary, presbytery, and personal libraries. I would like to thank Eugene Ensley, pastor of Peace Presbyterian Church, Clearwater, Florida, for permitting me to use his personal collection of General Assembly *Minutes*; and John Anderson, Executive Presbyter of Santa Barbara Presbytery, for permitting me to use the collection of *Minutes* in his office.

6. Joseph Lewis, ed., *Ingersoll the Magnificent* (New York: Freethought Association, 1957), pp. 237, 137.

7. Margaret Deland, *John Ward, Preacher* (Boston and New York: Houghton, Mifflin, 1888; repr. Ridgewood, N.J.: Gregg Press, 1967).

8. Quoted in *Minutes of the General Assembly of the Presbyterian Church in the United States* [cited hereafter in text as GA, PCUS], 1946, p. 169.

9. *A Digest of the Proceedings of the General Assembly of the Presbyterian Church in the United States, 1861–1965* (Atlanta: Office of the General Assembly, 1966), p. 254; *Minutes of the General Assembly of the Presbyterian Church in the United States of America* [cited hereafter in text as GA, PCUSA], 1914, p. 226; GA, PCUSA, 1932, p. 85.

10. See Smylie, " 'Of Secret and Family Worship': Historical Meditations, 1875–1975," p. 98; *Digest,* p. 254; GA, PCUSA, 1914, p. 221.

11. The southern church endorsed national prohibition in 1914, though several commissioners protested the action as an unwarranted case of intermeddling with civil affairs (GA, PCUS, 1914, pp. 71, 80b), but the following year the General Assembly strongly reaffirmed the traditional posture of the denomination concerning political issues (GA, PCUS, 1915, p. 29). No southern General Assembly ever pronounced on the issue of prohibition again.

12. For example, in 1889 it urged that petitions be sent to Congress in favor of a federal law prohibiting most kinds of Sun-

day work (*Digest,* p. 249); in 1895 it commended "all wise legislation for the protection of the Sabbath" (*Digest,* p. 250); in 1913 it congratulated President Wilson for closing the White House to pleasure seekers on Sunday (*Digest,* p. 251); in 1914 it rejoiced in the new law closing first and second class post offices on Sunday (GA, PCUS, 1914, p. 41), in 1938 it endorsed a proposal that the U.S. Post Office use "Observe Sunday" as a cancellation stamp during the Easter season (GA, PCUS, 1938, p. 66); and in 1941 it asked President Roosevelt to reduce the duties of military personnel on the Lord's Day "to the measure of strict necessity" (GA, PCUS, 1941, p. 169).

13. GA, PCUS, 1931, p. 157; GA, PCUS, 1973, p. 284; GA, PCUSA, 1914, p. 219; GA, PCUSA, 1949, p. 361; GA, PCUSA, 1951, p. 402.

14. A recent work on Sunday closing laws, for example, does not mention the Lord's Day Alliance or provide even the barest sketch of its history between the first decades of the nineteenth century and the present. See David N. Laband and Deborah Hendry Heinbuch, *Blue Laws: The History, Economics, and Politics of Sunday-Closing Laws* (Lexington, Mass.: Lexington Books, 1987).

15. One such law, passed in 1912, was the closing of all first and second class post offices on Sundays. See GA, PCUSA, 1951, p. 402.

16. For example, it called for "the enactment of a strong Sunday law for the District of Columbia" (GA, PCUSA, 1926, p. 57) and for the elimination of public service announcements and commercial advertising over the radio on Sundays (GA, PCUSA, 1935, p. 103).

17. In the early 1920s both denominations abolished their permanent committees on the Sabbath and turned their work over to other committees. See Weeks, "The Scriptures and Sabbath Observance in the South," p. 274.

18. GA, PCUS, 1939, pp. 116–117. This report is unusually thoughtful and perceptive and its reflective tone contrasts with the shrillness of many of the previous reports and the reports submitted after 1941, when the Permanent Committee's composition had changed once again.

19. GA, PCUSA, 1942, p. 196. The more pressing business at hand, to which the committee devoted most of its energies for the next several years, was laying the foundation for a "just and durable" peace for the postwar world

20. GA, PCUSA, 1942, p. 87. In 1942, the General Assembly not only assured the Lord's Day Alliance of continuing financial support, it invited the Alliance's General Secretary to make a short address, and it began the practice of printing the annual report of the Alliance in the Supplement to the Assembly Minutes, a practice that would continue until the denomination severed all ties with the Alliance in 1963 (pp. 88, 308–311).

21. Minutes of the General Assembly of The United Presbyterian Church in the United States of America [cited hereafter in text as GA, UPCUSA], 1960, p. 358.

22. GA, UPCUSA, 1963, p. 206. The committee did not go on to urge Presbyterians to cease all efforts to affect law and public policy. It specifically reaffirmed the traditional view of northern Presbyterians that the church may make theologically grounded claims on the state (p. 215), but it did not reconcile this continuing commitment with its principle that "moral convictions peculiar to a religious body ought not be imposed on the general public by law" (p. 206).

23. No overtures concerning the action on Sunday closing laws were received, though in 1964 five overtures were presented that asked the General Assembly to reconsider the church-state document as a whole. The General Assembly took no action on the overtures (GA, UPCUSA, 1964, pp. 41, 42, 323).

24. The General Assembly's refusal either to reestablish the committee or to fund the Lord's Day Alliance in its benevolence budget reflected a renewed commitment after 1914 to the doctrine that the church must not intermeddle in civil affairs. The record is clear that the Lord's Day Alliance did so intermeddle.

25. On two occasions during this final five-year period, the General Assembly declined to approve all parts of the committee's report. Although the rejected parts were not printed in the *Minutes,* it is very likely that they contained recommendations the Assembly considered too burdensome (see GA, PCUS, 1944, p. 163; GA, PCUS, 1945, pp. 94–95).

26. Whereas the northern church severed its relations with the Alliance in 1963, the southern church remained affiliated until reunion twenty years later. But relations between the southern church and the Alliance were not invariably smooth. In 1956 the General Assembly asked the Permanent Committee on Interchurch Relations to study the question of whether the denomination should continue its affiliation. The following year the Assembly approved the committee's recommendation that it

should be continued but that the Board of Managers of the Alliance should be informed of "certain unfavorable criticisms . . .
to the effect that the program of the Alliance has become 'archaic'
and its methods lack freshness and vigor." (GA, PCUS, 1957, p.
65). In 1958, the Ad Interim Committee on the Lord's Day also
recommended continued affiliation in view of "recent improve-
ments" in the Alliance's publications and work (GA, PCUS,
1958, p. 187). See note 30 below for an additional example of
strained relations between the southern church and the Alliance.

27. In 1957 the Permanent Committee warned of "the moral
and spiritual disaster to the churches and the nation which would
follow the complete secularization of the Lord's Day" (GA,
PCUS, 1957, p. 162).

28. In this regard it is instructive to note that the committee
reported: "Our study of the Word of God . . . has made it unmis-
takably plain that the wholesome and regular observance of the
Lord's Day is indispensable to a God-pleasing and God-sustained
life," and its neglect in modern times is "nothing less than a
tragedy in the life of the Church" (GA, PCUS, p. 182). See
Weeks, "The Scriptures and Sabbath Observance in the South,"
pp. 277–281, for an insightful review of the committee's report.

29. Just how dead the issue really was, even for conservatives
in the southern church, can be seen by examining the list of
charges against the General Assembly drawn up in 1973 and
transmitted to it by the General Assembly of the National Presbyterian Church (now the Presbyterian Church in America). The
list includes the ordination of women and the relaxation of the
rules calling for total abstinence and restricting the remarriage of
divorced persons, but it makes no mention of the General Assembly's new custom of doing business on Sunday (GA, PCUS,
1974, p. 27).

30. The complaint lodged by the Lord's Day Alliance
prompted the Permanent Committee on Interchurch Relations to
reexamine the denomination's ties with that organization. After
consulting with its General Secretary, an understanding was
reached, on the Assembly's terms, that allowed these ties to continue, which in fact they did until 1983. The report on the in-
cident stated that "our General Assembly recognizes that the
Lord's Day is not one to be marked only by prohibitions, but is a
day dedicated to the worship and service of the Lord. Since the
General Assembly is gathered for these very purposes, we have
affirmed to the Alliance that no distinction can be made as to

what part of the Assembly's docket is appropriate for Sunday" (GA, PCUS, 1970, p. 202).

31. The northern General Assembly never conducted official business on Sunday, and neither, to date, has the General Assembly of the reunited church.

32. I will document these observations in "From Old to New Agendas," in Milton J Coalter, John M. Mulder, and Louis B. Weeks, eds., *The Confessional Mosaic: Presbyterians and Twentieth-Century Theology* (Westminster/John Knox Press, forthcoming).

33. I am indebted to Langdon Gilkey for suggesting this very useful term.

5: Black Presbyterians and Their Allies

1. Vincent Harding, "Black Power and the American Christ," in *The Black Power Revolt,* ed. Floyd B. Barbour (Boston: Porter E. Sargent, 1968), p. 86.

2. John W. Lee, "Forty Years of Council Activity," *Africo-American Presbyterian,* November 22, 1934, p. 1.

3. Black Presbyterian and Congregational clergy met at Central Presbyterian Church in Philadelphia on October 28, 1857. It was evidently their second meeting. Elymas P. Rogers, moderator of the previous meeting, presumably in 1856, preached the sermon. Present at this meeting were eight Presbyterian clergy and five laymen, and three Congregational clergy—one from Massachusetts and two from Connecticut. (*Minutes and Sermons of the Second Presbyterian and Congregational Convention*; New York: Daly, 1858.)

4. Lee became pastor of First African on January 20, 1901, when the membership was only 48. By 1907 he had increased the membership to 225 and had made a substantial contribution to what was called that year the Presbyterian Council of Ministers and Laymen. (Brochure of the *14th Annual Meeting of Presbyterian Council of Ministers and Laymen, October 24–28, 1907*; Presbyterian Historical Society, Philadelphia.)

5. Lee, "Forty Years of Council Activity."

6. Alfred A. Moss, Jr., *The American Negro Academy* (Baton Rouge, La.: Louisiana State University Press, 1981), p. 19.

7. See, for example, such titles as "Is Presbyterianism Adapted to the Masses?" by Dr. W. A. Alexander, and "Social Purity—Some Helps—Some Hindrances," by Mrs. Caroline V. Anderson, at the meeting in 1900; or "The Supreme Purpose of the Church

as Expressed in the Gospels," by Rev. L. Z. Johnson, D.D., and "The German Gymnasia Versus the Laxity in Training of Colored Youth," by Rev. Matthew Anderson, D.D., at the Council meeting in 1916.

8. Moss, *The American Negro Academy,* pp. 16–31.

9. Henry J. Ferry, "Racism and Reunion: A Black Protest by Francis James Grimké," *Journal of Presbyterian History* 50/2 (1972), 77.

10. Carter G. Woodson, ed., *The Works of Francis J. Grimké* (Washington, D.C.: Associated Publishers, 1942), vol. 1, *Addresses,* pp. 239–240, 268–269, 506; Grimké to the Presbytery of Washington City, October 4, 1908, ibid., vol. 4, *Letters.*

11. Interview with Rev. Thomas J. B. Harris, December 21, 1988.

12. Andrew E. Murray, *Presbyterians and the Negro: A History* (Philadelphia: Presbyterian Historical Society, 1966), p. 230.

13. Ernest Trice Thompson, *Presbyterians in the South,* vol. 3 (Richmond, Va.: John Knox Press, 1973), pp. 84, 89; and "Continuity and Change," an unpublished, undated manuscript in the Woodruff Library Archives, Atlanta University Center.

14. Personal correspondence, Bryant George to Gayraud Wilmore, August 4, 1988.

15. Interview with Thomas J. B. Harris, December 21, 1988.

16. Cited in C. James Trotman, "Matthew Anderson: Black Pastor, Churchman and Social Reformer," *American Presbyterian,* 66/1 (Spring 1988), 19.

17. *Minutes of the 57th Annual Session of the Presbyterian Council of the North and West, October 4–8, 1950.*

18. *Monday Morning,* January 20, 1947.

19. Memorandum, John Dillingham to L. Charles Gray, November 19, 1953.

20. Ibid.

21. Personal correspondence, L. Patrick to Gayraud Wilmore, February 8, 1989.

22. B. Douglas Brackenridge, "Lawrence W. Bottoms: The Church, Black Presbyterians and Personhood," *Journal of Presbyterian History* 56/1 (Spring 1978). See also Thompson, *Presbyterians in the South,* vol. 3, p. 423.

23. Lawrence W. Bottoms, unpublished address to a conference with PCUS ministers, February 19–21, 1958, in the Woodruff Library Archives, Atlanta University Center.

24. Thompson, "Continuity and Change," p. 13.

25. Interview with Joseph L. Roberts, February 24, 1984.

26. Jesse B. Barber, *Climbing Jacob's Ladder* (New York: Board of National Missions, PCUSA, 1952), p. 92. A major feature of this program was the annual Lincoln University Summer Conference, which brought together Black and white clergy and laity for race relations training.

27. Interview, Jovelino Ramos with Kenneth G. Neigh, October 25, 1983, in *COCAR & CORAR Legacy, 1963–1987* (New York: New York Based Council on Church and Race, 1987), pp. 537–559 (limited edition in the archives of Johnson C. Smith Seminary, Atlanta).

28. *Minutes of the General Assembly of the UPCUSA,* Part I: *Journal,* 1963, p. 141.

29. The Black Presbyterian Leadership Conference of the PCUS was established at the 1969 General Assembly as an agency of the Assembly by recommendation of the General Council. Its purpose was to "recapture the historical Black experience so that the Black Church may work more concretely for the liberation of all Black people, move toward Black ecumenicity and work for world-wide Black unity so that Black people may be in a stronger position to challenge the white church with the truth of the gospel, and thereby usher in more quickly the day of authentic reconciliation among all the peoples of the world" (*Annual Reports of Assembly Agencies* [PCUS, 1970], pp. 17–18).

30. Joseph L. Roberts credits John Anderson, executive of the Board of National Missions of the PCUS, for opening the way for the BPLC and the Commission on Church and Race. The 110th General Assembly received a recommendation to recognize an independent Black caucus called for in a BPLC paper, "Black Expectations," adopted by the caucus in Atlanta on September 28, 1969 (see *Minutes of the General Assembly,* [PCUS, 1970], p. 151). This action was understood to supersede the previous recommendation from General Council. The caucus headquarters was established in Tuskegee, Alabama. Lawrence F. Haygood, Calvin Houston, Zeke Bell, Michael Elligan, and W. D. Tolbert were key leaders in the founding of the Leadership Caucus. In the UPCUSA the white allies at the national level were William Morrison, Kenneth Neigh, Eugene Carson Blake, Marshall Scott, and Clifford Earle. Among those most active in the founding of Black Presbyterians United (BPU) one year before the BPLC was created were Edler Hawkins, Bryant George, J. Metz Rollins, Robert P. Johnson, E. Wellington Butts, and J. Oscar McCloud. See J.

Metz Rollins, "The Spirit of Black Presbyterianism: Part II," *Periscope 2* (New York: Program Agency, UPCUSA, 1982), pp. 25–29.

31. "Profile of the Presbyterian Interracial Council," membership application brochure, 1964, in the Woodruff Library Archives of Atlanta University Center.

32. *NOW,* Newsletter of PIC, April 1964, p. 2.

33. See reports of COCAR in *Minutes of the General Assembly of the UPCUSA,* Part I: *Journal,* 1964, pp. 325–329; and *Journal,* 1965, pp. 394–402.

34. PIC was organized at the Des Moines Assembly for the purpose of mobilizing white support for the Concerned Presbyterians' proposal for a national race relations agency related to the General Assembly. Kenneth Waterman, its first executive, wrote in *NOW* (April 1964), "Commissions will work conservatively and quietly *within* the power structures of the establishment of the church. PIC will organize large numbers of frustrated individuals (most of them laymen) into a movement to work *upon* the establishment, as well as to militantly witness to and help the Negro community gain justice in all areas of civic life." But by 1967 the coalition was in decline. James A. McDaniel, Associate for Poverty and Community Organization of the Board of National Missions, wrote in *NOW* (Summer 1967), "Presently many PIC Chapters are 'paper' organizations, poorly financed and peopled by half committed members. Some chapters, when they hold meetings, are not large enough to require a room larger than a phone booth. Unable to harness the potential resources of their constituencies, PIC cannot at present produce much worth coalescing with."

35. For a study of the origin of these groups, their documents and contributions to theological renewal in the Black church, see Gayraud Wilmore and James H. Cone, eds., *Black Theology: A Documentary History, 1966–1979* (Maryknoll, N.Y.: Orbis Books, 1979).

36. Angela Davis was a twenty-seven-year-old Black militant and former philosophy instructor at UCLA. A member of the Communist Party in the United States, she was charged with murder, kidnapping, and criminal conspiracy resulting from a shoot-out in a San Rafael, California, courtroom in August 1970 that resulted in the deaths of Superior Court Judge Harold Haley, Jonathan Jackson, William Christmas, and James McClain. Davis was charged with supplying the guns used by the three prison-

ers. A codefendant, Ruchell Magee, was charged with firing the shotgun that killed Judge Haley. She was captured in a New York City motel and extradited to California, where she spent almost a year in prison and was finally exonerated after a sensational trial that galvanized the support of many Blacks and liberal whites who admired her courageous witness in behalf of civil rights and prison reform, but doubted that she could get a fair trial without the vigilant intervention of progressive forces across the nation.

37. Text of remarks by the Rev. Edler G. Hawkins to the 183rd General Assembly of the United Presbyterian Church U.S.A., Rochester, N.Y., May 24, 1971, in *COCAR & CORAR Legacy, 1963–1987: The Angela Davis Papers* (New York: New York Based Council on Church and Race, 1987), p. 2 (limited edition; in the archives of Johnson C. Smith Seminary, Atlanta).

38. James J. Cochran, Executive Vice President of The Presbyterian Lay Committee, Inc., to J. Henry Neale, co-chair of the Council on Church and Race, November 27, 1972 (The Angela Davis Papers).

39. "Why Angela Davis?" (draft of the National Race Staff of the UPCUSA response to the protest, pp. 12–13; The Angela Davis Papers).

40. News release of the Presbyterian Office of Information, New York, June 15, 1971.

41. The Black Manifesto of the Black Economic Development Conference (BEDC) was presented on May 15, 1969, to the 181st General Assembly in San Antonio, Texas, by James Forman. It called for reparations of over $500,000,000 to be paid to Blacks for centuries of enslavement and exploitation from which the churches and synagogues of the nation derived enormous benefits. Although the Assembly did not respond directly to Forman's demands, it did vote certain extraordinary measures by recommendation of COCAR. The Standing Committee on Church and Race said of the Manifesto: "We accept this new way of speaking to us, to affirm that it may be a necessary mode of God's coming to judge and to help to free us from racial attitudes that demean us." Each of the program boards, in specific terms, was called upon to make new funds and properties of the church available "in response to the critical needs that our brothers [of BEDC and La Raza, the Hispanic caucus] have focused for us." The report was adopted by the General Assembly. One of the consequences was the creation, by the 182nd General Assembly (1970) in Chicago, of a National Committee on the Self-Development of Peo-

ple to design criteria and allocate thousands of dollars to "local communities of need" through judicatory self-development committees. See Arnold Schuchter, *Reparations: The Black Manifesto and Its Challenge to White America* (Philadelphia: J. B. Lippincott Co., 1970); Robert S. Lecky and H. Elliott Wright, eds., *The Black Manifesto* (New York: Sheed & Ward, 1969); Gayraud Wilmore, *Black Religion and Black Radicalism* (Garden City, N.Y.: Doubleday & Co., 1973), pp. 202–210; *Minutes of the General Assembly of the UPCUSA,* Part I: *Journal,* 1969, pp. 660–681; *Journal,* 1970, pp. 667–676.

42. Edler G. Hawkins Papers, Woodruff Library Archives, Atlanta University Center.

43. For analyses African American theologians make of contemporary ecclesiology of the ecumenical movement, see David T. Shannon and Gayraud Wilmore, eds., *Black Witness to the Apostolic Faith* (Grand Rapids: Wm. B. Eerdmans Publishing Co., 1988).

6: Changing Understandings of Ordination

1. *New York Times* (February 12, 1989), pp. 1 and 14.

2. Edward Schillebeeckx, *The Church with a Human Face: A New and Expanded Theology of Ministry* (New York: Crossroad Publishing Co., 1985), p. 2.

3. These four tests are discussed in Max Thurian, *Priesthood and Ministry: Ecumenical Research* (Oxford: Mowbray, 1983), pp. 141–142.

4. Schillebeeckx, *The Church with a Human Face,* pp. 141–142.

5. Ibid., p. 66.

6. Ibid., pp. 116–117.

7. Ibid., pp. 119–121.

8. Ibid., p. 133.

9. Ibid., pp. 145 and 194.

10. Ibid., pp. 152–154.

11. Ibid., pp. 205–206.

12. Wilhelm Pauck, "The Ministry in the Time of the Continental Reformation," in H. Richard Niebuhr and Daniel Day Williams, eds., *The Ministry in Historical Perspectives* (New York: Harper & Brothers, 1956), p. 112.

13. Ibid., p. 113.

14. Ibid., pp. 129–131.

15. Ibid., pp. 138–141. The quotation is from Calvin, *Institutes* 4.3.16.

16. Ibid., p. 116.

17. Ibid., pp. 143–147.

18. Constant H. Jacquet, Jr., *Women Ministers in 1977* (New York: National Council of Churches, 1978). For a more detailed description of the movement of women into ordination in mainline Protestantism see Barbara Brown Zikmund, "The Struggle for the Right to Preach," in Rosemary Radford Ruether and Rosemary Skinner Keller, eds., *Women and Religion in America,* vol. 1: *The Nineteenth Century* (San Francisco: Harper & Row, 1981), pp. 191–241; and "Winning Ordination in Mainstream Protestantism: 1900–1965," in Rosemary Radford Ruether and Rosemary Skinner Keller, eds., *Women and Religion in America,* vol. 3: *The Twentieth Century* (San Francisco: Harper & Row, 1985), pp. 339–383.

19. "Pastoral Letter," *General Assembly Minutes* (1832), p. 378, quoted in Lois A. Boyd and R. Douglas Brackenridge, *Presbyterian Women in America: Two Centuries of a Quest for Status* (Westport, Conn.: Greenwood Press, 1983), p. 94.

20. Boyd and Brackenridge, *Presbyterian Women in America,* pp. 96–108.

21. Ibid., pp. 109–112.

22. Ibid., pp. 111 and 179–180.

23. See Ben M. Barrus, Milton L. Baughn, and Thomas H. Campbell, *A People Called Cumberland Presbyterians: A History of the Cumberland Church* (Memphis, Tenn.: Cumberland Presbyterian Church, 1972).

24. Boyd and Brackenridge, *Presbyterian Women in America,* pp. 126–138.

25. Ibid., pp. 153–155.

26. Hazel Foster, "Ecclesiastical Status of Women," *The Women's Pulpit* 40 (July–December 1964), 8.

27. William Baumgaertner, ed., *Fact Book on Theological Education 1987–88* (Vandalia, Ohio: Association of Theological Schools in the United States and Canada, 1988).

28. Maggie Ross, *Pillars of Flame: Power, Priesthood, and Spiritual Maturity* (San Francisco: Harper & Row, 1988), p. 5.

29. Kenneth L. Woodward, "Feminism and the Churches," *Newsweek* (February 13, 1989), pp. 58–61.

30. Maggie Ross, *Pillars of Flame,* p. 28.

31. See Jean Baker Miller, *Toward a New Psychology of Women*

(Boston: Beacon Press, 1976); Nancy Chodorow, *The Reproduction of Mothering* (Berkeley, Calif.: University of California Press, 1978); and Carol Gilligan, *In a Different Voice: Psychological Theory and Women's Development* (Cambridge, Mass.: Harvard University Press, 1982). See also Mary Field Belenky, Blythe McVicker Clincy, Nancy Rule Goldberger, and Jill Mattuck Tarule, *Women's Ways of Knowing: The Development of Self, Voice and Mind* (New York: Basic Books, 1986).

32. See note 31.

33. Christina Robb, "A Theory of Empathy," *Boston Globe Magazine* (October 16, 1988), pp. 18–19, 42ff.

34. Lynn Rhodes, *Co-Creating: A Feminist Vision of Ministry* (Philadelphia: Westminster Press, 1987), p. 114.

35. Davida Foy Crabtree, "Empowering the Ministry of the Laity in Workplace, Home and Community: A Programmatic and Systemic Approach in the Local Church" (Doctor of Ministry project, Hartford Theological Seminary, 1988), p. 98.

36. William F. May, "Vocation, Career, and Profession," a paper presented at "To Serve the Present Age" (A Consultation on Evangelicals and American Public Life sponsored by the Institute for the Study of American Evangelicals, November 17–19, 1988), typescript, pp. 3 and 6.

37. May, "Vocation, Career, and Profession," pp. 10–15.

38. Ibid., pp. 18–19.

39. Ibid., pp. 25–26 (emphasis added).

40. *The COCU Consensus: In Quest of a Church of Christ Uniting* (Princeton, N.J.: Consultation on Church Union, 1985), paragraph 25 (emphasis added).

41. A summary of the Professional Ethics Group findings was prepared by Maura Tucker, "Women in Ministry: Sexual Ethics," a typescript available from the Center for Ethics and Social Policy, Graduate Theological Union, Berkeley, Calif., 1988.

42. Rita Nakashima Brock, *Journeys by Heart: A Christology of Erotic Power* (New York: Crossroad Publishing Co., 1988).